Constance Legaigneur

Le Ther d'Amboise

LA V
CHARLES

Député au Corps Législatif.

24 rue de Rivoli

Avocat

Membre du Conseil Général de l'Yonne

7, RUE DE LA PAIX

Mme David

née de Grignon

Fernand

Mme C. Parlange

Le Cher
d'Amboise

Henri de Buffo

Avocat

M. Jules Levita

Boyve

Henri de
Fleurieu

Docteur en Droit.

Mr BYRON KIRBY.

Attaché à la Légation

Fernand Varin d.

Montaigne

aux États-Unis d'Amérique

24 rue de Rivoli

Beaumont

Mr de Boyve

Madame de Tornant.

RON KIRBY

Constance Legaigneur

Eugene Le Comte

Le Ther d'Amboise

Député au Corps Législatif.

24 rue de Rivoli

Membre du Conseil Général de l'Yonne

Avocat

Avocat

7, RUE DE LA PAIX

Mme David

Fleurieu

née de Grignon

Fernan

Mme C. Parlange

Le Cher

Henri de B

7, RUE DE LA PAIX

Avocat

M. Jules Levita

C. Parlange

de Fleurieu

Docteur en Droit.

Le Cher
d'Amboise

Mr BYRON KIRBY.

Attaché à la Légation

Creole Thrift

REGAN

An Imprint of HarperCollinsPublishers

Creole Thrift

Premium Southern Living Without Spending a Mint

ANGÈLE PARLANGE

PHOTOGRAPHS BY WILLIAM WALDRON

HarperCollins books may be purchased for educational, business, or sales promotional use. For information please write:
Special Markets Department, HarperCollins Publishers Inc., 10 East 53rd Street, New York, NY 10022.

For editorial inquiries, please contact Regan, 10100 Santa Monica Blvd., 10th floor, Los Angeles, CA 90067.

FIRST EDITION

Designed by Laura Klynstra

Photograph credits:
All photography by William Waldron, except:
Pages 32 and 33 by Joel Pickford; pages 19 (top) and 106 (bottom) by Joey Sedtal; pages 203 and 204 by Peter Vitale,
© *Veranda* magazine; pages 8, 10, 11, 12, 15, 17, 19, 20, 28, 38, 50, 66, 101, 105, 106, 107, 109, 125, 129, 154, 183,
and 192 courtesy of the Parlange family's collection; page 108 reprinted by permission of *National Geographic*;
page 104 by Smith, reprinted from *Holiday* magazine.

Illustration credits:
Pages 6, 7, 22, 88, 145, 147, 150, and 172 by Mark Andresen; page 89 by Diana Huff; page 165 by Mita Bland;
pages 112 and 128 by Dave Kelsey; pages 133 and 166 from the author's personal collection.

All original documents and archival material courtesy of the author's personal collection, except:
Page 136, cover of Circus Pony, reprinted by permission of G. Schirmer, Inc. (ASCAP);
page 123, cover of *The Whore's Rhetoric*, reprinted by permission of Astor-Honor, Inc.

Printed on acid-free paper

Library of Congress Cataloging-in-Publication Data
Parlange, Angéle.
Creole Thrift: Premium Southern Living Without Spending a Mint / Angéle Parlange ; with photographs by William Waldron.
p. cm.
ISBN 13: 978-0-06-078806-3
ISBN 10: 0-06-078806-2
1. Handicraft. 2. House furnishings. 3. Decoration and ornament—Louisiana. I. Title.
TT157.P3133 2006
747—dc22
2006046462

06 07 08 09 10 ❖ /RRD 10 9 8 7 6 5 4 3 2 1

For

Mama and Daddy

and my grandparents,

especially Mie

Contents

Introduction
AIN'T TIME A WRECKER

Lubertha Hurst was, and still is, a second mother to me. She reared my brothers, too, and ran our household for years. She was there when my parents came back from their Acapulco honeymoon. There when my oldest brother, Puffin, came home from Baptist Hospital in New Orleans. There when Brandon, my middle brother, arrived. And finally, on the third go-round, there for me. She chose to wear a uniform to work every day: a cornflower-blue dress with short sleeves bordered in white that hugged her plump brown arms. Every other day she alternated her shoes because she had corns on her feet. Whereas Mama created an imaginary world for us with fairies and elves as playmates, Lubertha brought order to our house. She loved to sweep, clean, and make her homemade bread called "light bread," along with pralines and fresh lemonade.

Every day, when I got home from the hour-long commute to grammar school, John Henry, who drove us to and from school in his olive-green LTD with brown vinyl top, dropped me off at Lubertha's house next door, rather than at home. I had supper with Lubertha and Mr. Jackson almost every evening. Mr. Jackson was Lubertha's live-in boyfriend who was always asleep on the sofa when he wasn't eating or working. Not until I was out of high school did I realize that he was actually passed out from too many Jax beers; Jax was a local brewery, now out of business. After roast, rice and gravy, and a fresh vegetable from her garden (cushaw was my favorite), Lubertha would teach me how to dance.

She had a 12-inch-square wooden board supported by springs and a rotator on which we practiced swiveling our hips. I never asked her where she bought it but surely it was purchased from a TV ad and paid C.O.D. Lubertha would play Barry White's "I'm Qualified to Satisfy You" on her turntable and we

MY MOTHER, LUCY PARLANGE

would get off the "hip twister" and swirl our legs and arms on her linoleum floor. I never thought of it then, but our afternoon sessions laid the groundwork for the invitations I receive now, the reason I'm invited out so often to go dancing.

❧ ❧ ❧

One day, when I was in junior high, two of my parents' friends, Miss Daiseybelle and Mr. Percival, came over to our house for toddies—what other people call drinks. Lubertha served them bourbon and branch water (that's what my mother calls our artesian well water), in Mama's monogrammed silver beakers. Miss Daiseybelle and Mr. Percival had attended my parents' wedding and had children who commuted to school with us.

"Lucy, I'd love to see your wedding book," Miss Daiseybelle said to Mama, "and that precious baby scrapbook you made for Angèle. Is it within reach?"

"I'll see if I can unearth them," Mama replied. "I know where our wedding album is, but I'm not sure about that baby scrapbook. I think Brandon stored it in the shed. He's always throwing out things of mine that he doesn't think are important."

Mama left the gallery, returning about a half hour later with both books. Miss Daiseybelle stacked the books on her lap and Mr. Percival gazed over her shoulder.

"I didn't realize I was smoking those Pall Malls that long ago," Mr. Percival said. "I thought that habit kicked in during grinding season." He owned a sugarcane mill in Pointe Coupée Parish.

"Oh, there I am in my shirred aqua dress I had borrowed from Sister. I didn't tell her and she got so mad with me the next day. I think it was because she wasn't invited to the wedding," Miss Daiseybelle laughed.

"Lucy, you were aptly named 'Bride of the Camellias' because you and Skipper are one good-looking couple."

FROM RIGHT: ME, JIMMY CLAYTON, KENNY HURST, CLAUDE HURST, AND MY BROTHER, BRANDON PARLANGE

Fonville Winans, a brilliant Southern photographer, took all the old Southern family wedding portraits until he died in 1996. He won a prize for my mother's bridal portrait, which he titled "The Bride of the Camellias." For Mama's January wedding, all of her cousins brought camellias from their gardens for the flower arrangements and the bridesmaids' bouquets. My mother interspersed "white perfections" on the Belgium-lace hem of her wedding dress, too.

Mama put my baby book on top of the wedding album. "I love the cover of this baby book, Lucy. Did you paint this?" Miss Daiseybelle asked Mama.

"I did. But you should see Puffin's. I really knocked myself out for his scrapbook."

"Oh, don't you look adorable here holding Angèle at the front gate," she said.

Lubertha passed another round of toddies and peered over Miss Daiseybelle's shoulder at the photograph. "Uh uh uhm, ain't time a wrecker," she said.

Mama cut her eyes at Lubertha as if to say, *curb it*. The rest of us looked at each other with an almost snicker and yet dared not let my mother see us. Lubertha almost always told the truth.

Lubertha rarely complained, except about her weight. She was always saying, "I'm trying to reduce," rather than, "I'm on a diet." She was also the secretary of T.O.P.S., or **T**ake **O**ff **P**ounds Sensibly. On Wednesdays she left work early and went to the T.O.P.S. meeting followed by the NAACP rally.

Last August, I went home for the weekend. Before I saw my family, I went to Lubertha's new place, a government-subsidized apartment in New Roads, a nearby town. She moved several years ago. The apartment is arranged almost like her old house. Martin Luther King's and Bobby Kennedy's portraits still hang above the tan vinyl sofa. I remember that those pictures were on layaway forever at Bill's Dollar Store; I even rode to Bill's with Lubertha to make her last payment.

Lubertha looked good, but she had developed a few wrinkles on her forehead. We talked about her family and her health before I shifted gears.

"What I remember is getting up on that dance board and doing the twist with you. Do you have any new jigs?" I asked.

"I broke my hip last year and I couldn't do the twist if Bobby Kennedy asked me to dance. *Ain't time a wrecker?*"

CREOLE EXPRESSION:

"He/she fell out," a very Southern expression used when one is overwhelmed.

Part One

HERITAGE

I grew up in Louisiana on a plantation, which has been a major influence on my design business. Parlange on False River was built circa 1750. It is considered the oldest plantation in Louisiana and is a rare example of French colonial architecture. A National Registered Historic Landmark, Parlange has remained in my family for eight generations—unusual in America. Most people think of plantations built in massive Greek Revival style like Tara in *Gone with the Wind*, but Parlange was built earlier and, at least in the interior, is not nearly as large. Architects and historians celebrate it for its lovely galleries (galleries encircle a house whereas verandas and porches don't) and the exquisite hand-carved architectural features like the fanlight windows and intricately detailed hand-carved cypress mantelpieces, chair rails, and ceiling moldings. Many plantations were burned during the Civil War or changed hands because the families did not have the means to save them. The trials and tribulations of saving Parlange never daunted my great-great-grandmother. Her passion and love for the house surpassed the daily fear of losing it and imbued in the next generations

17

the same sense of devotion and pride in preserving the house and its history. We all feel such great respect and love for Parlange. It is a magical place and setting enlivened with personalities, tragedies, and blessings, and all who know it feel a connection with her. I think about it everyday—how it shapes my perspective on life, but at the same time doesn't consume me. When I visit similar places in this country or the world, I experience the same feeling about history and the role it has played in people's lives and values.

DINING ROOM AT PARLANGE

DINING ROOM MANTELPIECE AT PARLANGE, CIRCA 1930

SALON AT PARLANGE, CIRCA 1930

SALON AT PARLANGE, CIRCA 1930

OPPOSITE: PORTRAIT OF MARIE VIRGINIE DE TERNANT AVEGNO. MARIE VIRGINIE'S DAUGHTER WAS
AMÉLIE VIRGINIE AVEGNO GAUTREAU, THE SUBJECT OF JOHN SINGER SARGENT'S *Madame X*. MY MOTHER ALWAYS
SAYS, "IF ONLY WE HAD THE *Madame X* PORTRAIT IT WOULD BE WORTH MORE THAN THIS WHOLE PLANTATION."

The house was, and still is, furnished primarily with period Louisiana and French furniture upholstered in gold and rouge satin brocades with complementary pieces from each successive generation. Eclectic as the furniture styles are at Parlange—early Louisiana armoires with simple, French-influenced lines, Boulle tables and cabinets from the 1800s, English furniture and portraits from my mother's family—so too is my heritage.

Fantasizing about the ancestors from my past inspired me to create and market my own line of eveningwear, decorative fabrics, and home accessories. But you don't have to grow up on a plantation, or descend from someone who came over on the Mayflower, to find inspiration for your home in unexpected places. The thing we all have in common is heritage. This chapter will show you how to use remnants of your own heritage—photographs, letters, deeds, or even an old football program—to recreate decorative pieces for your home.

MADAME X
BY JOHN SINGER SARGENT
Grand-daughter of Le Marquis de Ternant
Daughter of Mrs Avegno
Niece of Judge Charles Parlange
Portrait painted in Paris

I LOOKED BACK TO MY HERITAGE TO FIND INSPIRATION. EVEN THOUGH WE DON'T OWN THE *Madame X* PORTRAIT, I USED HER FAMOUS PROFILE AND THE BARBERINI BEE TO CREATE MY OWN DESIGN.

OPPOSITE PAGE: MY BATHROOM VANITY CHAIR UPHOLSTERED WITH MY MADAME X FABRIC DESIGN

Calling Cards

◈ ◈

We were participating in our favorite family pastime—sitting on the front gallery, telling stories, and admiring the view of False River. It wasn't Thanksgiving or Christmas or any holiday; there was no reason for my homecoming, which for me was a holiday in itself. We began talking about family memories and relics.

"Mie, whatever happened to those calling cards of Virginie's?" I asked my grandmother.

"Darling, I have those kept safely in the attic. I think they are under the west side dormer window."

I left my rocking chair and went on my search, reaching the dormer window by an indirect route. The pram from my strolling days was filled with dusty Beatrix Potter books and Madame Alexander dolls. I tripped on an old wooden tea caddy, and envelopes filled with cards fell on the cypress planks. Squatting down, there was just enough light for me to see that I had stumbled on the calling cards.

I sat on the dusty floorboards, mesmerized by all the cards alphabetized in miniature envelopes. I looked for "P" and found *Virginie de Ternant Parlange, 44 Rue de Luxembourg, Paris*. Virginie, my great-great-grandmother, had a salon in Paris where the intelligentsia—musicians, political figures, and artists—gathered for conversation. Upon arriving at the salon, they would leave their calling cards on a small oval silver tray in the vestibule. She spent half of the year in Paris, and the other half in Louisiana. Her card was engraved in beautiful script with a crown above her name.

Virginie's calling card seemed to be a symbol of all of the stories I had heard about her through Mie and other relatives. Her oil portrait is life-size, accentuating her piercing blue eyes and the flattering ringlets in her hair. In her black gown with ermine trim, Virginie seems as grand as her

Marius de Ternant

Charles Parlange

Mme C. Parlange.

Madame Parlange,
Rue du Luxembourg, 44.

LA VICOMTESSE CHARLES DE GRANDVAL.

Mme Virginie Ternant.

Mr Smith

17, rue de Miroménil.

Mr & Mme Anatole Avégno

Le Cher d'Amboise.

24 bis rue de P.

EDOUARD SEIGNOURET,

Mr & Mrs Smith

37 rue de l'Oratoire

La Comtesse de Mandelsloh.

Mr Jules Lévita,

Docteur en Droit.

Avocat.

66, rue N.le des Mathurins.

Mr MASON,

Envoyé Extraordinaire & Ministre Plénipotentiaire

des États Unis d'Amérique.

portrait. The stories of her taste for the Parisian lifestyle and her delight in transporting it back to her home in Louisiana always intrigued me.

Circular parlors were the rage in the 1840s, so Virginie was inspired to re-create a circular salon in her Louisiana home even though her parlor was square. In order to achieve this effect, she placed demi-lune tables in the corners of the room. Claude Debufe, a Parisian court painter, was commissioned to paint four children's portraits on oval canvases, which were then mounted in gilded oval frames. Virginie hung each portrait in the four corners of the room above the semicircular tables, thus creating the illusion of a circular salon.

Virginie's infatuation with Paris was put on hold with the outbreak of the Civil War. She now had to defend her land and her circular salon. As daunting as this was, Virginie still found a way to play Southern hostess. She organized barbecues and dinners for both the Northern and Southern troops, using her hospitality and charm to save her home from being destroyed.

As I went through the letters of the alphabet, I imagined her entertaining the owners of the calling cards. I went backwards from "P" to the beginning of the alphabet. I didn't know these people, but their cards were so beautiful I felt as if I did. Most were printed in black ink in different fonts of cursive script, and the card stock, although it was not engraved, was smooth and had a lovely patina. The "A" envelope had *Le Chev d'Amboise, 24 bis rue de Rivoli—Avocat*. What was "Chev"? A title? I knew "Avocat" meant *lawyer*. His card was printed in old French script and appeared more masculine than Virginie's. In the "L" envelope was *M. Jules Levital—Docteur en Droit*, Juris doctor. Mr. Levital's card was engraved in a tailored Roman type. The "G" collection contained a *La Vicomtesse Charles de Grandval, 10 Place Vendome*. Mme. de Grandval was royalty. In the "S" envelope I found *Mr. and Mrs. Smith*, whose card had a family crest and motto which read, *"Tu ne cede malis."* "Thou shalt not gossip" is the translation from old French. What a brilliant motto for this pair, much better than "Noblesse Oblige." This was my favorite one just because I found a bit of humor in it. Mr. and Mrs. Smith may not have, but I did.

OPPOSITE: VIRGINIE'S PORTRAIT AND THE OVAL-FRAMED PORTRAIT OF JULIE DE TERNANT IN THE "OVAL SALON"

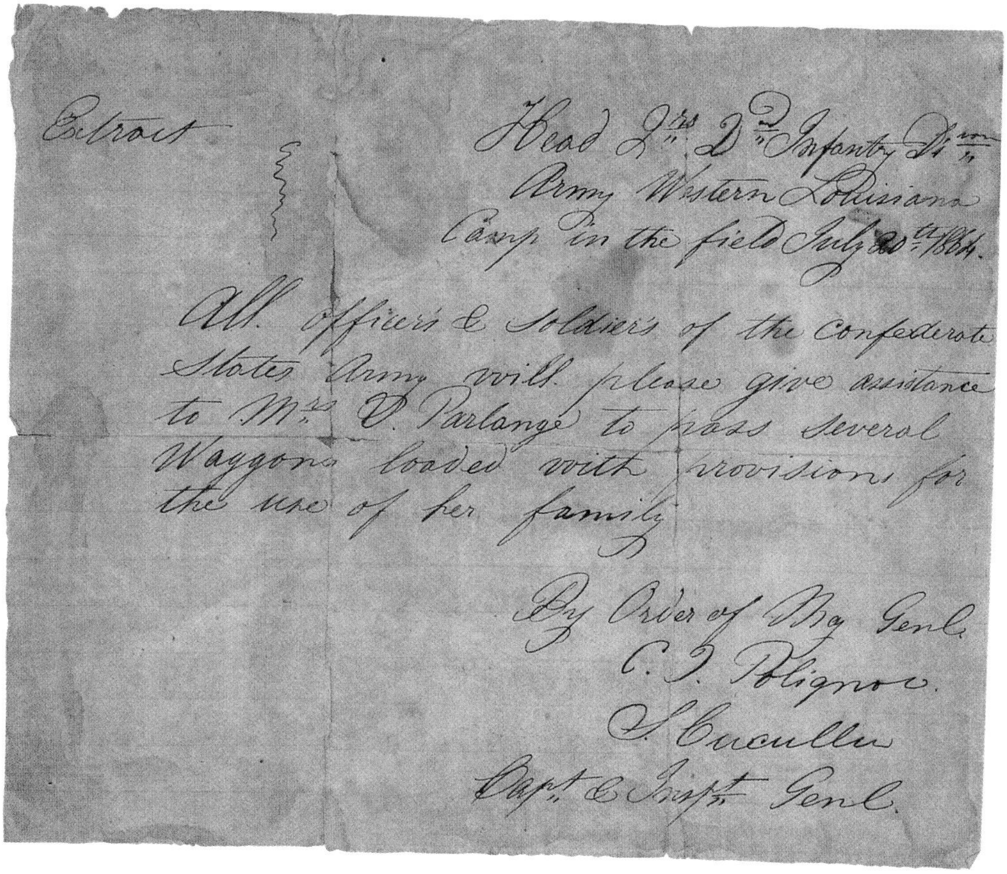

Extract

Head 2nd Division Infantry Division
Army Western Louisiana
Camp in the field July 20th 1864.

All officers & soldiers of the Confederate States Army will please give assistance to Mrs. V. Parlange to pass several Waggons loaded with provision for the use of her family

By Order of Maj. Genl.
C. J. Polignac.
S. Cucullu
Capt. & Inspt. Genl.

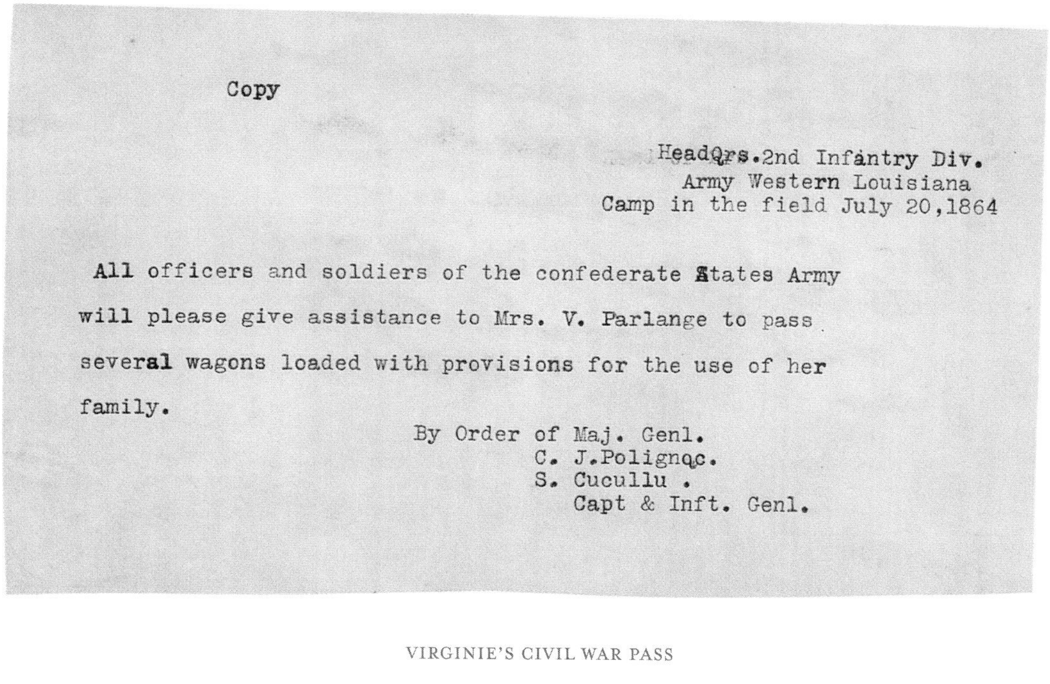

Copy

HeadQrs. 2nd Infantry Div.
Army Western Louisiana
Camp in the field July 20, 1864

All officers and soldiers of the confederate States Army will please give assistance to Mrs. V. Parlange to pass several wagons loaded with provisions for the use of her family.

By Order of Maj. Genl.
C. J. Polignac.
S. Cucullu.
Capt & Inft. Genl.

VIRGINIE'S CIVIL WAR PASS

OPPOSITE: I NOW KEEP THE CALLING CARDS IN A TEA CADDY ON MY MANTELPIECE

Virginie must have had an amazing collection of friends leaving visiting or calling cards. Some cards had bent corners, which meant that the callers had not found anyone home. Others were bordered in black, left by widows or widowers. Each one was distinctive to its owner and many of the addresses still exist in Paris today. I fantasized about the personalities and the lively conversations they must have had. To think that Virginie, an American, collected and organized such a wide array of friends really amazes me. Parisians are known for preferring to socialize with their own. Obviously, Virginie charmed and intrigued the old guard.

The light from the dormer was waning, but I couldn't stop examining the cards. I had to find some way to make these cards and their owners come alive. What could I do with them? I had it. I could arrange them in a design and print them on silk taffeta—the same material used in my eveningwear collection—in hues of magenta, fuchsia, and raspberry. The names would be in gold, a prettier contrast to the iridescent fabrics than the black ink of the cards. I would upholster Louis XV and XVI–style chairs with the printed fabric. The chairs would be fitting for a traditional salon setting and would make much more of a statement than mere yards of fabric. Now the voices of the calling cards could engage in conversation just like they would in a salon gathering.

⚜ ⚜ ⚜

A knock three times with a broom handle on the floor planks startled me. It was my father, using his method for waking me up for school when I was little. My room was above my parents' room so my floor was their ceiling. Now it meant, "Are you still in the attic?" No, I was in Paris at 44 Rue de Luxembourg, but I was coming back to Louisiana with something special.

MY FATHER, WALTER CHARLES PARLANGE, JR., IN FRONT OF VIRGINIE'S PORTRAIT

OPPOSITE: PORTRAIT OF JULIE DE TERNANT IN OVAL FRAME

Entertaining and Recipes

Bayside Plantation Mint Juleps
(from Peter Patout)

1 1/2 cups simple syrup *(see recipe on page 41; use while still warm)*
2 cups smashed and bruised mint
2 fifths bourbon
Mint sprig *(optional)*

1. Combine all the ingredients in a large bowl or pitcher and let marinate for at least 30 minutes. If desired, strain the mixture to eliminate the mint leaves.
2. Serve over ice and garnish with mint sprig.

Yield: 8–10 cocktails (Southerners) or more.

Note: I like to use a muddler. A silver one is beautiful for showmanship, but if you're making them with no one else in the kitchen, who cares.

OPPOSITE: MY FATHER AND I,
AT OUR BIRTHDAY FETE

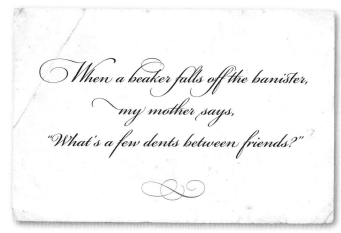

*When a beaker falls off the banister,
my mother says,
"What's a few dents between friends?"*

CHEESE RIBBONS (FROM HENRI MOORE OF LAFAYETTE, LOUISIANA)

1 pound extra-sharp cheddar or baby Swiss cheese, grated

1 1/2 sticks butter

2 cups unbleached plain flour

1 1/4 teaspoons baking powder

1/2 teaspoon salt

1/2 teaspoon Tabasco

1/2 teaspoon cayenne pepper

1. Allow the cheese and butter to become room temperature before starting. Preheat the oven to 300°F.
2. Sift the flour once in a medium bowl. Add the baking powder and salt, re-sift, and set aside.
3. In a separate bowl, mix the butter and cheese together with your hands. Add the Tabasco, cayenne pepper, and flour mixture. Mix well.
4. Lightly grease a baking sheet. Use a cookie press to squeeze out the mixture in rows along the entire length of the cookie sheet. Space the rows about 1/2 inch apart.
5. Place the sheet into the oven and bake for 15 minutes. Lower the heat to 225°F and bake for 15 or 20 minutes, or until crisp. About 5 minutes before the baking is complete, use a pizza cutter to divide the ribbons into 3-inch strips. Serve hot or let cool for 20 minutes. This recipe freezes well.

Note: Cooking time varies from oven to oven. If you think the ribbons are baking too fast, leave the oven door open.

Yield: about 120 3-inch ribbons.

OPPOSITE: MY GODDAUGHTER, CAROLINE LUDWIG

THE PATIO AT PARLANGE, THEN...

AND NOW

(MY BROTHER) BRANDON'S MILK PUNCH

1 2/3 cups cream

5 cups milk

2 cups simple syrup (see recipe below)

3 cups sugar

3 tablespoons vanilla

A fifth of bourbon

Sprinkle nutmeg on top

SIMPLE SYRUP:

3 cups sugar

1 1/2 cups water

TO MAKE THE SIMPLE SYRUP:

Add the sugar and water to a medium-size saucepan. Bring to a boil and let simmer undisturbed for 2 minutes. Cool before using.

NOTE: Simple syrup is great to have on hand and you can refrigerate it for later use.

TO MAKE THE MILK PUNCH:

Add all the ingredients in a large bowl, then transfer to a pitcher. Serve neat or over ice.

Tip I LIKE TO PUT MILK PUNCH IN THE FREEZER FOR ABOUT 6 HOURS FOR AN ICIER EFFECT.

Recipe For

PLACE CARDS (A BIT LIKE PLAYING PAPER DOLLS BUT WITHOUT A CHANGE OF CLOTHES)

Ingredients

CARD STOCK THICK ENOUGH TO STAND UP ON ITS OWN (2 PLY IS IDEAL), SCISSORS OR X-ACTO KNIFE, GLUE. CRYSTALS (SMALL OR 3 MILLIMETERS FLAT BACK, AVAILABLE IN SELF-ADHESIVE ALSO), FELT, FABRIC, OR WRAPPING PAPER SCRAPS, COLORED PAPER, NARROW RIBBON, METALLIC TWINE, OR LEATHER CORDING, GOLD METALLIC PEN

1. *Find images that you like or that match the personalities or interests of your guests. For my Leo zodiac birthday party, I made paper dolls that represented my father and me. My father's doll was dressed with his trademark hat and mine with a dress and pocketbook. Every guest (gentleman or lady) received either my father or me.*

2. *Photocopy an image (the simpler the better) that you like, or modify a picture to your taste and size it to about 6 1/2 inches tall and 2 to 3 inches wide.*

When you enlarge and reduce on a photocopier it gives you the complementary height or width. The doll should be about 6 1/2 inches tall.

3. *Trace the outline of the doll onto black (or whatever color you prefer) card stock, adding 1 inch at the bottom of the doll for the plinth. This will be the stand or pedestal (all guests are important) so that the place card can stand upright.*

4. *Cut the doll out with scissors or an X-acto knife. Score the bottom pedestal so that it will bend neatly to stand.*

5. *Embellish lady dolls by gluing on crystals for their necklaces. Cut out 1 1/2- by-1-inch pieces of card stock for their handbags. Decorate the handbags using scraps of material and make handles for the bags out of ribbon.*

6. *Decorate the male dolls' hats with colored paper and ribbon, twine, or leather cording for the band.*

7. *Write each guest's name on his or her doll's pedestal with a gold metallic pen.*

GUESTS LOVE TO TAKE THESE DOLLS HOME WITH THEM AS A REMEMBRANCE OF THE PARTY, AND, IN MY CASE, THEIR LEO HOST.

Everybody Looks Good in Sepia Tones

The curtains in my sunroom were burlap bare. They had to come down but I just hadn't gotten around to doing it. I was having a drinks party, which is always the ultimate deadline for me. Much, much more threatening than a leaking roof or gutters. As usual, I had procrastinated. Two weeks before, I was in the throes of the first stages of getting ready: ordering the liquor and barmen and designing the invitations.

The next step was to move the "store-file" boxes from my bedroom to my inner sanctum: my closet and dressing room. There were no horizontal spaces left in my house for framed pictures, but I had boxes full of photographs that were mostly stashed at the foot of my bed. One box piqued my interest. It was layered with old family and childhood pictures, with an icing of roach droppings. Every time I stumbled on it, I got mad; not at the roaches, but at my laziness. While moving other boxes that contained items like Condé de Caralt (cheap, delicious champagne), and Mississippi Cheese Straws (nonperishable leftovers from a previous party), I had a collision with the roach box. The contents flew all over the room—broken frames and glass, dust, string, K&B No. 2 pencils, and loads of old photographs.

I began to clean up. Once I vacuumed off the roaches' graffiti, my present was the photos. Who were these people? We had to be related but there was no identification. One lady was wearing an amethyst necklace to die for, the same necklace that my mother borrowed from my cousin Belle for her wedding. But what I really wanted to know was what brand of aftershave the lady used—she seemed to be sporting a mustache.

There was a picture of Lubertha, my nanny, and me. Another of my brother babysitting Nibbs, my golden retriever. There was no sequence, no order. But the photographs had one thing in common:

MY FATHER

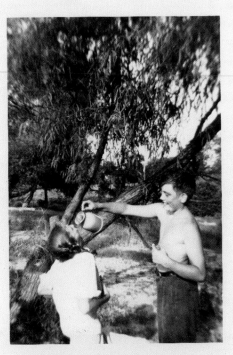

"POURING IT ON"; MY MOTHER AND HER
COUSIN, MERWIN BRANDON

MY MOTHER WITH FRIENDS

MY BROTHER AND MY DOG, NIBBS

they were keepers. I had to show them off. After all, *everybody looks good in sepia tones*. Even snaggletoothed cousins.

I laid the photos out on the floor with other mix-and-matches to amuse myself. There must be something I could do with these other than put them in frames. An ex of mine used to tell me that I'll take over any horizontal space. He was right.

⚜ ⚜ ⚜

The disparity between my French and English relatives tickled me, perhaps because I had lined them up next to one another knowing that there'll always be a bristle between those two cultures. My French relatives with their huge families (my grandmother was one of twelve) and their brunette good looks saddled right next to the same generation of blond-haired, blue-eyed future in-laws. Oh, how that patriarchal great grandfather Brierre would have disdained my English relatives for having only seven children! Out of sheer mischief, I had to create a way that they could all be together.

Perhaps I could copy these photos, make iron-on transfers, and apply them to fabric so that all the ancestors were side by side. I could live in the present and be in the past at the same time. My yoga instructor always tells me, "You're in the moment on purpose," when I'm upside down in a headstand. I was in the moment, on purpose.

I asked one of my favorite Kinko's employees, Joyce Brashears, if she could do iron-on transfers. Joyce had been in the T-shirt business prior to working at Kinko's and still had the equipment. "Joyce, I need to transfer about fifty photographs onto cotton sateen. Do you think you could manage that with your machine?"

"I'll give it a shot," she said. All I had to do was buy the fabric, position the photographs, and determine the length. A cinch.

Cotton sateen would not compete with the photos; instead it would appear like a cardboard mat surrounding each picture; plus it's inexpensive. I made the photocopies, changing some of the sizes so that the layout worked. The size of each piece of fabric (two windows) was 5 feet by 10 feet. Joyce used silk pins to secure the pictures on the cotton, rolled the fabric up, and told me to give her about ten days.

A week later, Joyce called. She was having trouble getting the photos ruler-straight. I told her to let me see if the unevenness bothered me. Just before dusk, we met and rolled the fabric out on my front lawn. My mother calls my yard a postage stamp, and she's right; we spilled onto the sidewalk. The irregularities were so slight that I may not have noticed had Joyce not pointed them out to me. "Joyce, you're a genius," I said, giving her a big hug.

"The only problem was keeping it on the ironing board and off the kitchen floor," Joyce said. "Those kids of mine never clean up after themselves."

Joyce charged me one hundred and fifty dollars for the job. I gave her an extra twenty-five for a tank of gas and a heavy-duty mop.

"Thank you, sweetie. I've got a full tank but I'm gonna buy some fresh catfish with this at Barrow's. I won't have to worry about the grease splattering tonight. Let's make something else."

Bordered in silk dupioni, these panels would become my new draperies. Imagine that, curtains that could make me laugh and cry. Now all I had to do was pick out the silk dupioni color to border these panels. Khanh Tran, my seamstress, would tell me the yardage for the border and curtain ties. She'd be thrilled to make something as simple as a border rather than a shirred dress.

I hopped in my Jeep and headed to Joanne's Fabrics on Veterans Boulevard in the New Orleans suburbs. My playwright friend calls Veterans the "Boulevard of Dreams" because every store imaginable exists: Party Circuit, Payless Shoes, The Chatta Box, Home Depot, and my addendum, Frost Top. I called Khanh, who told me that the border would take 8 yards of fabric. If the dupioni was still priced at eleven dollars a yard, that would be eighty-eight dollars.

Joanne's was jam-packed with shoppers buying purple, green, and gold fabric, boas, and sequins for Mardi Gras costumes. The dupioni aisle was free and clear and I had my pick of luscious colors. Crayola "blue-green" caught my eye. This shade would complement my collection of black-framed forties wallpaper designs, which have sea-foam and pale aqua hues. After Joanne's, I stopped at Home Depot to buy plain, brushed-steel curtain rods. And, at last, to Frost Top for a root beer float.

⚜ ⚜ ⚜

It took Khanh no time to put the border and ties on the photo panels. They looked great in their silk mat. My friend Winn came over to help me hang them, and with her help, the curtains hung perfectly. Act two was over.

"Reach in the icebox, Winn, and pop that birthday present of mine."

"You mean the Veuve Clicquot in the meat drawer?"

"You got it. It's intermission time and the drink's on me."

After several glasses of champagne, the piercing eyes of the mustachioed lady started to follow me around. The tour guide in every canned antebellum plantation tour always says, "…and you can tell if it's a good portrait, because if you move across the room, his or her eyes will follow you."

Was she watching me or just scanning the room for a can of Burma-Shave? Surely she was happy with her family reunion.

Mustache and all, *everybody looks good in sepia tones…*

"…even a snaggletoothed relative."

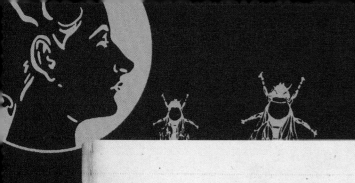

Recipe For
"EVERYBODY LOOKS GOOD IN SEPIA TONES"

BLACK-AND-WHITE OR COLOR PHOTOGRAPHS, STRING FOR MEASURING, STICKY NOTES, WHITE COTTON SATEEN, STRAIGHT PINS, SISAL OR ROPE TWINE, SILK DUPIONI OR OTHER MATERIAL FOR THE BORDER (OPTIONAL)

1. *Gather your favorite photographs.*

2. *Determine the size of the curtain and measure an outline on the floor using string. Place the photographs within the measured space. Decide which photographs you will use and what sizes are needed (i.e., original size, enlarged by 50 percent, reduced by 25 percent, etc.). Put a sticky note on each photo stating the desired size and make photocopies of the photographs.*

3. *Buy a piece of white cotton sateen (any fabric store should carry this), adding 2 inches on each side to the desired size of your curtain.*

4. Place and straight-pin the photocopies onto the fabric in the desired positions. Roll or fold up the fabric and bring it to a silk screener. If you want to "frame" the panel of photographs, use a fabric of your choice (I chose silk dupioni) and desired width for the border. Most fabric store clerks can help determine the fabric amount needed if you tell them your desired finished size.

5. Look in the yellow pages for custom-made T-shirt shops or silk screeners. Explain your project to the company clerk. My suggestion: Ask in person, not over the phone.

6. Once the silk screener has printed your photo-panel, look in the yellow pages for "Tailors, alterations." Ask the tailors if they are capable of sewing a border on the specific size of your panel. Again, it is always best to bring your project to the shop to explain your ideas in person.

Tip

Oftentimes, I like to use upholstery or drapery fabric for pants and jackets. It has a great weight and the patterns are architectural or graphic rather than the usual fashion designs. On the other hand, I prefer to use dress fabrics and trims for curtains and tiebacks. Dress fabric can be backed and lined to give it added weight for upholstery. The fashion fabric colors are also much more vivid and bold, and are less expensive since their width is usually 45 inches rather than 54 inches, the decorating standard.

THE TULANE VS. LOUISIANA STATE UNIVERSITY SHOWER CURTAIN

✦ ✦

Cousin Belle left all her valuable furniture and letters to her nephew Peyton. He was the only male heir and she wanted him to have first choice of the contents from her family home, Arcole, in Pinckneyville, Mississippi. Now it was my cousins' and my turn to go through the house and pilfer through the leftovers. I headed to a wooden filing cabinet. It was more of a piling cabinet, as there were no alphabetized separators, just stacks of musty papers. Rifling through deeds, land grants, and family trees, I suddenly came across the Tulane vs. Louisana State University football program. Why was the football program in the midst of these more serious documents?

I studied team players dressed in knickers-style trousers, horizontal-striped socks, and shirts that looked like they had inspired The Gap. It seemed to be from the 1930s. *Woodward, Tulane, Quarterback, Weight, 152, Height, 6 even, age 19, first year on team.* He looked like he could throw a serious ball. On the same page was an ad for "Izzy Wolf's Smoke House, 5 cent cigar, Always good," and "Jacobs Candy,

made last night." A player named "Big Hog" Baysinger wore a coat over his letter sweater that looked like my fake shearling. He appeared limber enough to do a flip-flop despite his nickname. I would've had a crush on him but I don't know if I could deal with kissing someone called "Big Hog."

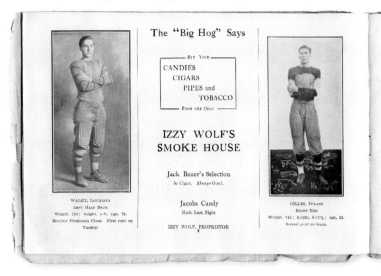

Also pictured: *Williams, "Shorty" Brandon, 6' 4", weight 210, Cheerleader, Voted most popular male at Louisiana State University*. He was my great-uncle and the one who most likely saved this program. Uncle Shorty was the most popular uncle to all of us cousins, too. My favorite photograph was of Joe Daigre, "The Rubber," carrying a pail and towel. Joe was the masseur; I might have tried out for the team if I could have gotten a backrub from him.

JOE DAIGRE
Rubber.

⚜ ⚜ ⚜

I pictured re-creating this program. Where would the team gather besides the football field? I had it—in the locker or shower room. Maybe I could assemble the team photographs on white cotton as they appeared in the book to make a shower curtain. It would be the first time I'd ever taken a shower with two college football teams.

First I had to think of someone to help me with this project. I remembered that there is a T-shirt shop in the mall that silk-screens photographs on XXL tees, like the ones with a photo of an infant with an arrow beneath it pointing downward. Surely a T-shirt shop could silk-screen more than one photograph.

I drove across the Greater New Orleans Bridge to Oakwood Mall, which has many shops providing unusual services and gifts. As I exited onto Terry Parkway, there before my eyes was a listing for "Cindy's Tee's and Things" on the Oakwood Mall marquee. Also advertised on the mall marquee was a shop called "Rings and Things," and another one that piqued my interest: "Primarily Purple." It's always a good sign, too, when there's a Perfumemania and a Sunglass Hut. In addition, there was a Hancock's, where I could buy cotton sateen.

⚜ ⚜ ⚜

I bought the white cotton (about 3 yards to make a shower curtain) at Hancock's and then walked the mall until I saw "Cindy's Tees and Things," a free-standing kiosk centered midway in the mall. Miss Cindy, the proprietor (she wore a custom nametag that I'm sure she made), manned her own booth. I told her about my project. She replied that she had never silk-screened on a large length of fabric, but she could screen the photos on mugs and to-go cups for me.

"No thank you," I told her. "That's not what I had in mind."

I pleaded with her and insisted that my special project could be executed just like her T-shirt applications. The only difference was that multiple photos would be copied from the program. I wasn't even asking her to do both the JV and varsity teams, just my favorite players and advertisements. She agreed to tackle the star players and told me to come back in a week.

⚜ ⚜ ⚜

One week later, I was back at "Cindy's Tees and Things." Miss Cindy had made transfers of the photos and had ironed them onto the fabric just as she did to her mugs, to-go cups, and tees. She had accomplished my request and had even transferred the sepia color of the aged program. Miss Cindy was beaming with her success and told me she would start offering this product to her customers. She had enjoyed the challenge and was excited to offer something more unique than mugs.

Harry's Ace Hardware was my next stop. I bought some twine and made ties so the photo-screened fabric could hang as a shower curtain. Sewing the twine ties onto the shower curtain was much easier than sewing a button on a dress. Two quick stitches for each of the nine ties. I hung it in my lavender bathroom. It was exciting to have all those boys at my beck and call.

Miss Cindy enlarged Joe Daigre, "The Rubber," at my request, and repeated his picture several times—the chorus. Joe had the brightest smile and I wanted to honor him. He was in heaven, and eternalized, without having to rub another sweaty back.

After all, he had gotten a promotion to my own private bathroom.

COL. THOS. D. BOYD
President Louisiana State University.
Vice-Pres. Third Dist. S. I. A. A.

TULANE

LOUISIANA VARSITY

TOP ROW—(Left to Right)—Moseley, Mgr.; Sayes, Crawford, Kleck, Howell, Halligan, P. D.; Dutton, Evans, Johnson, C.; Gosserand, Coach Dwyer
MIDDLE ROW—McHenry, Potts, Capt. Thomas, Whitehead, Hightower.
BOTTOM ROW—Spencer, E.; Spencer, G.; Dupont, L.; Reily, Dupont, J.; Hall, Johnson, M.; Walet, Wade.

26

Recipe For
"THE TULANE VS. LOUISIANA STATE UNIVERSITY SHOWER CURTAIN"

FOOTBALL, BASKETBALL, OR ANY OTHER SPORTS PROGRAM,
STRING FOR MEASURING, WHITE COTTON SATEEN FABRIC,
STRAIGHT PINS, SISAL OR ROPE TWINE

1. *Pick your favorite first- and second-string teams and any other entries.*

2. *Determine the size of the shower curtain and measure an outline on the floor using the string. Determine how many photocopies you will need to fill the measured space.*

3. *Photocopy the desired program pages and repeat some if you don't have enough or like some selections better than others.*

4. *Buy a piece of white cotton sateen (any fabric store should carry this), adding about 2 inches on each side to the desired size of your shower curtain. Most*

fabric store clerks can help determine the fabric amount needed if you tell them your desired finished size.

5. Place and straight-pin the photocopied program pages onto the fabric in the desired positions. Roll or fold up the fabric and bring it to a silk screener.

6. Buy some narrow rope or sisal twine at a hardware store.

7. Look in the yellow pages for custom-made T-shirt shops or silk screeners. Explain your project to the company clerk. Ask in person, not over the phone.

8. Look in the yellow pages for "Tailors, alterations." Ask if the tailors can sew a straight seam on the shower curtain as well as nine evenly spaced rope twine ties to the top edge for hanging on the shower rod. Again, it is best to explain this simple job in person.

Mr. Will Wyatt

Fredonia

Ky.

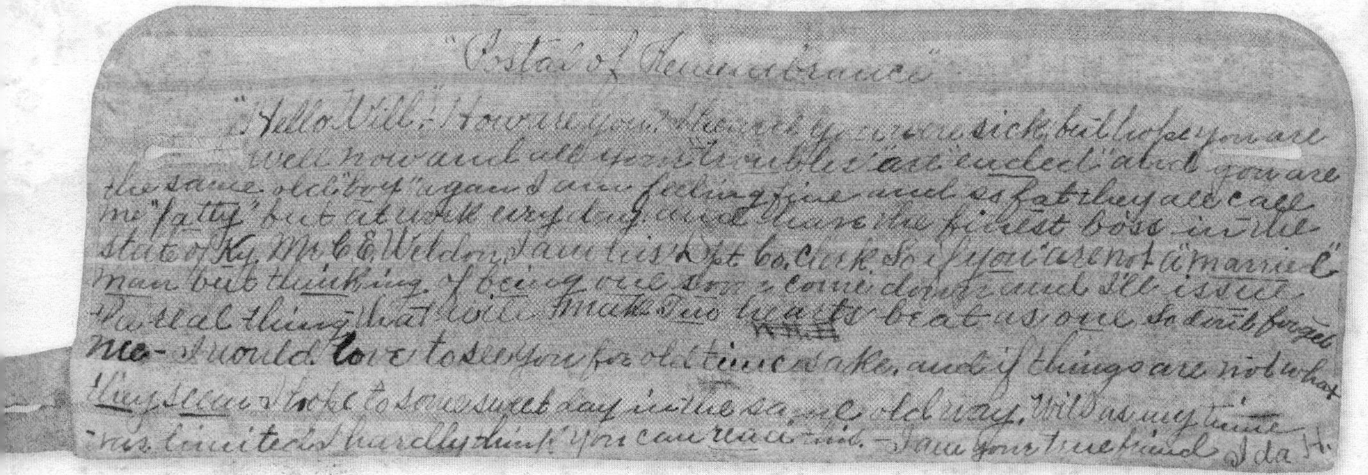

"Postal of Remembrance"

"Hello Will, How are you? I heard you were sick, but hope you are
well now and all your troubles all ended. I am the same old "boy" again. I am feeling fine and so fat they all call
me "fatty" but at work every day and have the finest boss in the
state of Ky. Mr. C.E. Weldon. I am busy at 6 o clock. So if you are not a "married"
man but thinking of being one soon come down and I'll give it
the real thing. What will make Two hearts beat as one. So don't forget
me. I would love to see you for old time's sake, and if things are not what
they seem. I hope to some sweet day in the same old way. Will as my time
is limited I hardly think you can read this. I am your true friend Ida H.

MISS IDA'S RULES

Miss Ida Hazard did not play by *The Rules*. She invented her own set, her own way. It was February 3, 1907, and she put herself down in print—something my mother told me never to do. Unlike most who put pen to paper, Miss Ida was a bit more inventive. She starched a French cuff belonging to her friend, Will Wyatt, and stated her intentions loud and clear. Next she stamped it, took it to the Marion, Kentucky, post office, and sent it to Mr. Will Wyatt in Fredonia, Kentucky. This is what she wrote:

Postal of Remembrance

> "Hello Will" How are you? I heard you were sick, but hope you are well now and all your "troubles" are "ended" and you are the same old "boy" again. I am feeling fine and so fat they all call me "fatty" but at work everyday and have the finest boss in the state of Ky., Mr. C. E. Weldon. I am his Dept. Co. Clerk. So if you are not a "married" man but thinking of becoming one soon come down and I'll issue the real thing that will make two hearts beat as one. So don't forget me. I would love to see you for old time sake, and if things are not what they seem, I hope to some sweet day in the same old way. Will as my time was limited I hardly think you can read this. I am your true friend. Ida H.

What I'm wondering is, what was Miss Ida doing with Mr. Will's French cuff? I didn't know that in 1907 people spent the night out and left their baggage behind. I asked my friend John Hazard, Miss Ida's great nephew and the one who inherited the cuff, but he told me that he wasn't there and couldn't report.

Well, Miss Ida knew what she was up to and her solicitation came to fruition. Mr. Will came around, and whether she was a fatty or not, he proposed. Now that is much better than asking someone to marry you at a Saints football game.

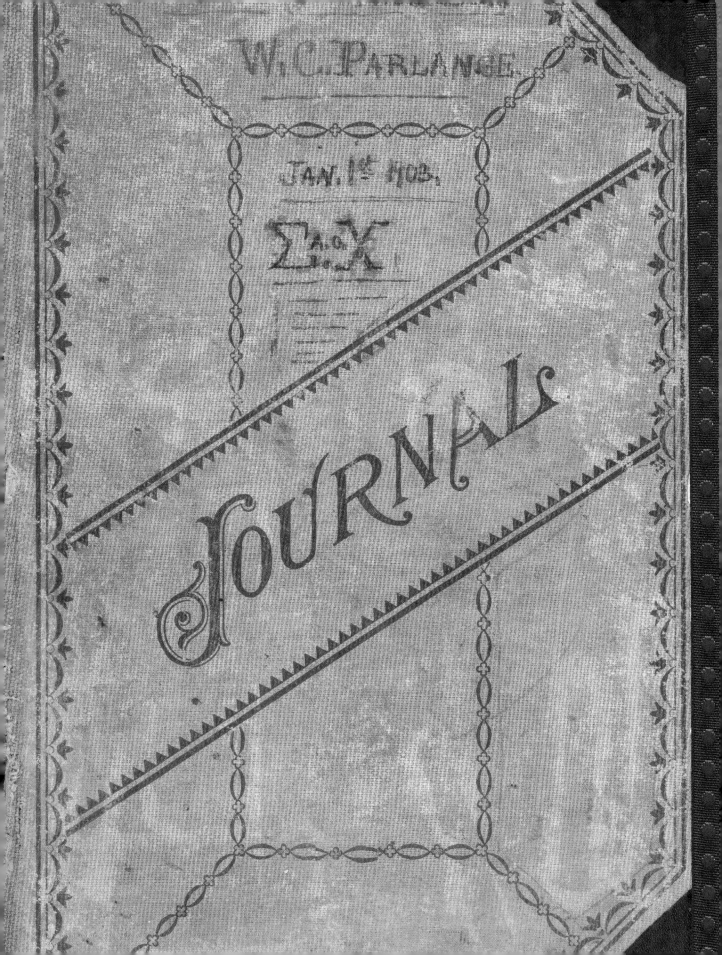

W. C. PARLANGE.

JAN. 1st 1908.

Σ.A.O.X

JOURNAL

FRENCH 75

Mie, whom you know by now, was my grandmother and lived in the big house with us; she always told me my grandfather's middle name was "Girls." He was christened Walter Charles Parlange but his fraternity brothers called him "Girls." I knew Pops was plenty popular, good-looking, and had lots of girlfriends, but it wasn't until recently as I was cleaning and reorganizing the bookcase at Parlange that I found out some things about Pops on my own.

The library at Parlange is wonderful. It is considered a typical "Southern Gentleman's Library" and shows that people were reading the same books that were currently being read on the Continent. Louisianians knew more about what was happening in France than they do today. It was the first time I had ever gone through the bookcase quietly, thoughtfully, and with French wax to polish the books along the way.

First editions of *Uncle Tom's Cabin*, law books of my great-grandfather and grandfather, *History of the Social Life*, *History of the Intellectual Life*, DeQuincey's Works—*Romance and Extravaganzas*, Owen's *Homer's Illiad*, *The Parisians*, *Philosophie des Gens du Monde*, *The Federal Judge*, *History of Louis XIV*, *The American Boy's Handy Book* (a favorite), and that old musty paper smell lured me. I loved looking at the front of the books, imagining to whom they belonged, and examining the handwritten date they were given or received. Behind and somewhat hidden from the good books, I found brochures from old-fashioned resorts like Mountain Top in Maine and the White Mountains of New Hampshire where family members must have vacationed. Then there were farm ledgers and cotton and sugarcane crop year-end tallies. One was a ledger written in Pops' handwriting from 1903 which especially interested me. Leafing through it, I found his French lessons and his essays on books he'd read. Pops went to the University of Virginia and then to Tulane Law School. Although

MY GRANDFATHER, POPS (BACK ROW, FAR RIGHT),
AND HIS FRATERNITY BROTHERS

he was quite the scholar, he also captained the rugby team and made time for dances and organizing parties. I flipped to the back of the ledger where I found the real lessons on life: several pages of his semester social engagements noting whom he was escorting to each. This was much better than any Black Book I'd seen. There were ruled columns with girls' names like "May Boullemet . . ." another column stating who was escorting her (May was always being escorted by Pops, it seemed), and a third column naming either the event or the dance: the "two step, t.s.," or "waltz, w." In the margin on the left was a space that was either left blank or inserted with "married." This comment was noted next to the names of maidens who were no longer available. It seemed that Pops must have really been crazy about May; as he stated in an affirmation at the bottom of one page: "Freshman (Newcomb) Class play—whenever it is, <u>must take</u> May Boullemet." I'm sure he did.

Each girl had a number next to her name, and after reading three ruled pages of Pops' dates, I started to wonder where Mie was. After all, she was the one who ended up marrying Pops. A few pages further along, and counting, number 72, number 73, number 74, and last but not least, number 75, was "Paule Brierre," Mie's maiden name. There she was. She was the very last entry. No other entries followed.

I rushed into the kitchen to tell my mother what I had found. She said, "Well, I'm not surprised. Mie always told me, 'I'm still pinching myself that I caught Walter, Sr.'"

"I know, but what do you think about number 75 out of 75?"

"Well, were there any entries after her?" Mama grinned with delight.

And that's what happens when you find Miss Right.

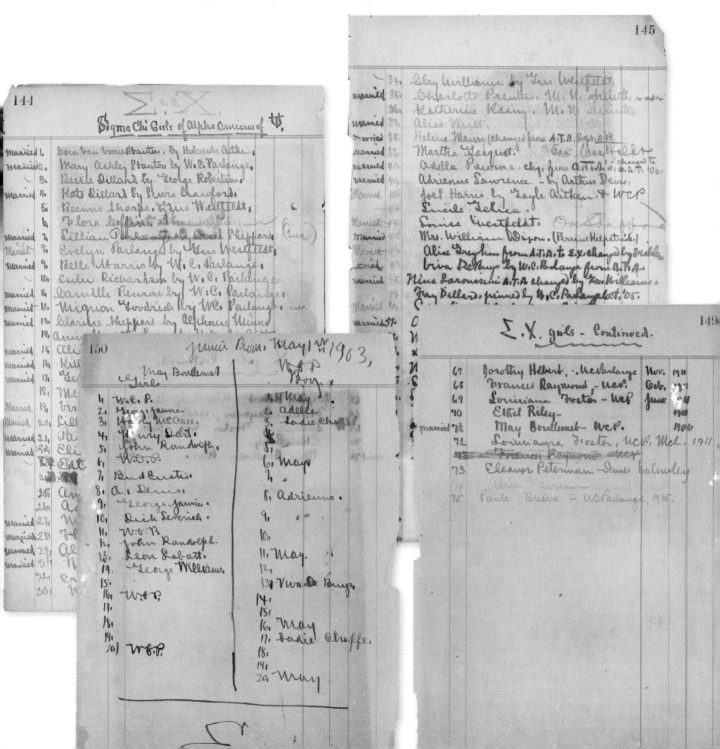

May you live long and
many pickles
the man
And marry who has the
most nickles

Guess who

A NICKEL'S ADVICE

⟶✠ ✠⟵

Cousin Belle Brandon was born in 1889 and was reared on Arcole Plantation, Pinckneyville, Mississippi. Because there were no formal schools in Wilkinson County, Cousin Belle was sent to St. Katherine's in Bolivar, Tennessee. As a going-away gift, Belle was given an autograph book to take with her to boarding school. The first autographs and well wishes began at the Arcole dining table, with family and cousins inscribing their sentiments to Belle. After my unexpected discovery of the keepsake in the Arcole library, it felt to me like I'd found a buried Civil War money chest. Unlike any ordinary guest book, this one was pale-pink with deckle-edged pages and a lovely cover made of something resembling a porcelain doll's face— china-like with a faint filigree design. It was pretty and unusual. The autograph book and Arcole's wonderful library were about all that was left after the only named-male Brandon heir got everything, including the house and most of its contents.

I seem to be drawn not to the big brown furniture, but to the letters and books of my forebears. I could tell this little diary was something special. And Cousin Belle Brandon was a treasured friend to all of her fellow schoolmates and relatives.

Upon opening the porcelain-like cover and flipping through the book, I found another generation's flourishingly neat penmanship expressing poetic affection. None of our present-day distractions were mentioned. Each page was autographed by one friend with a remembrance to Cousin Belle:

> *My dear Belle,—Aim above morality, be not simply good. Be good for something. Your loving*
> *music teacher, Edna Foukier, St. Katherine's School. Bolivar, Tenn. December 14, 1903.*

Another one reads,

> *Whenever you see a monkey climbing a tree—think of me rather, your cousin, Lane.*

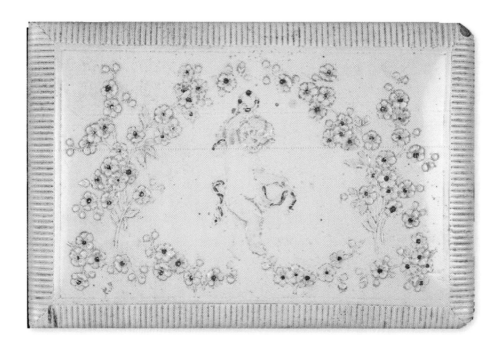

But the autograph that was my favorite was,

May you live long and eat many pickles, and marry the man who has the most nickels, Guess who.

Belle didn't heed "Guess who's" advice and ended up being a "maiden lady." That's what my grandfather always called her and other ladies in that generation who didn't marry. It was a much more civilized description than "spinster" or "old maid." But Belle had a wonderful life and it was just like she was married. She and her brothers—Robert, Lane, and Gerard—lived together at Arcole. Cousin Belle supervised the meals and made sure Arcole wasn't a bachelor pad. None of the brothers ever married either. In those days, there just weren't many people around to date who weren't your cousins.

Even though Belle dismissed eating pickles, I knew I had to do something with this marvelous remark on life. And so I did.

⚜ ⚜ ⚜

Once again, I was off to Kinko's to meet up with Joyce Brashears. She had told me to call her when I had another project and I definitely had a good one. But this time, since the saying wasn't very long and the subject not so serious, I decided on just a plain pillow. Wouldn't a small pillow copied exactly from Cousin Belle's diary with a black passementerie trim be a perfect statement on my sofa?

"That's easy, sweetie," Joyce said to me, upon hearing my request. "I even think Kinko's will let me do that here while I'm on break. Plus, I can easily stitch that right up for you with that trim of

yours. I've got some cotton sateen left from those curtain panels I screened. Just buy me a little poly-foam, not that old goose down, so it'll keep its shape and you can still read about those pickles and nickels."

All I had to do this time was get a small pack of Hobbs Bonded Fabrics brand polyester foam ($3.89) uptown at the Quilt Cottage on Nashville Avenue. I wouldn't have to trek out to Joanne's in Metairie. Of course, that would mean I'd miss out on a root beer float, my usual treat after Joanne's. But a Mochassippi (New Orleans' local version of a Starbucks' mocha frappaccino) at CC's, just down the block from the quilt shop, would be Joyce's and my reward. I always give myself a reward before I begin a project, not at the end. It motivates me.

⚜ ⚜ ⚜

One day later, I met Joyce at PJ's coffee shop, next door to Kinko's on Tchoupitoulas Street, while she was on break. The pillow and project were all sewn up.

I placed it dead center on my aqua sofa, and I've taken up the cause and advice of *Guess who*.

So may you live long and eat many pickles and marry the man who has the most nickels.

*May you live long and eat many pickles,
And marry the man who has the most nickels.
Guess who.*

Recipe For
"A NICKEL'S ADVICE"

Ingredients

AN AUTOGRAPH BOOK, DIARY, JOURNAL, OR LETTER,

WHITE COTTON SATEEN, TRIM, RIBBON, OR SEAM BINDING,

POLYESTER OR DOWN PILLOW FORM

1. Photocopy the page in the book, journal entry, or letter.

2. Buy a piece of white cotton sateen, adding about 2 inches on each side to the desired size of your pillow. Buy trim, ribbon, and whatever else you want to finish the edges. Seam binding works well, too, and comes in many colors. Buy

a pillow form (polyester or down) to fit the size of your photocopy. The clerk can help you with the size if you are unsure.

3. Look in the yellow pages for custom-made T-shirt shops or silk screeners. Explain your project to the company clerk. My suggestion: Ask in person, not over the phone.

4. Once the silk screener has printed your photocopy onto the cotton sateen, look in the yellow pages for "Tailors, alterations." Ask the tailors if they are capable of making a pillow with straight seams and trim. It is always best to bring your project to the shop and explain your ideas in person.

Part Two
THE BIG BROWN FURNITURE
CAME IN THE MAIL

It's big, brown, and in the way.

As nice as it is to inherit mementos or furniture from a relative, or even an old friend, it doesn't necessarily mean it's good or good-looking. It might just be awful. My mother always asks me where I put my great-aunt Rosine's secretary.

"It's in the warehouse," I tell her.

"But it belonged to your favorite aunt."

"I know and I think I was the last one to be contacted about her personal belongings."

Almost every family ends up having to divide the big brown furniture. Even if there's only one piece. My friend Lindy Boggs says of her pieces like these, *"The big brown furniture came in the mail."* This chapter explores how to think about a piece in a different light—what I call reappraisal, or for the politically correct, recycling.

Then there's roadkill: questionable furniture and curiosities other people throw out by the roadside for the lucky collector. Both the big brown furniture and the roadkill can be transformed into kicky new pieces. An afternoon with spray paint, carpenter's glue, and a little ingenuity can turn into a delightful and productive day. This section shows how you can reinvent the past through your furnishings.

A CONVERSATION PIECE

⤙⤛ ⤜⤚

Since my brother will inherit Parlange, my mother often asks me if there is anything in the house that I would like. Then, once she gives it to me, she always says, "Now don't let anybody see you taking that and don't tell anybody. I'll wrap it up in newspaper and put it in your trunk." Does she think I'm crazy or what? I wouldn't dream of telling anyone, especially my brothers.

Recently, my mother phoned me in New Orleans with her usual offer. What my New Orleans dining room needed was a large, antique gold-leaf mirror. Five were hanging at Parlange so I figured that losing one wouldn't make that much difference.

I took a drive up to False River from New Orleans for the mirror inspection. After having a look around the house, I thought the Louis XV mirror in the Blue Room, with its cracking gold-leaf patina and smoky mirror, would definitely look elegant over my French chest. Mama was sitting on the front gallery waiting for my selection. Opening the French doors from the Blue Room, I went outside to tell her that I had found something.

"Come with me," I said, holding Mama's hand as she got up from the wicker rocking chair, "and see what I've chosen." We walked inside and I pointed to the mirror over the cypress mantel. "This is the piece that I would like as your generous gift."

"Darling, you have to choose something other than the mirrors. They must stay in the house for historical reasons."

"But you told me I could have anything."

"Well, I didn't mean the portraits or the mirror," she said. "Surely there is something else."

OPPOSITE: THE ORIGINAL LOUIS XV MIRROR AT PARLANGE

79

There wasn't. I'd made up my mind, and being a stubborn Leo, I couldn't see the beauty in any other object.

My Polaroid camera, always with me, was in my Jeep. I went down the back stairs and got it. While I was snapping photos of the mirror, my mother asked what I was doing.

"I've got an idea brewing," I told her.

As I drove back on Highway 90 to New Orleans with my knee navigating the steering wheel, I pulled out my Palm Pilot and took my mobile phone out to make a call.

"Teenie, could you please be at my house tomorrow morning? I've got a project and will provide photos and a sketch for you. Take the street car uptown and get off at the Soniat Street stop and I'll meet you there. We'll walk back to my house. I've got the sizing, gold leaf, and an 8-foot ladder." Teenie was an English girl who gold-leafed for me. She would always oblige my urgent needs.

"Now what?" she asked. "I can be there by 11:00 A.M."

Touché!

When we arrived at my house, I put the Polaroids out on the table with a rough sketch of the mirror.

"Teenie, I want you to gold-leaf a likeness of this frame on the wall. I've already called Crasto Glass and ordered a 30-by-50-inch mirror. They'll deliver it tomorrow. The frame that you gold-leaf will surround the Crasto mirror. You can shade the frame in gray so that it appears to be three-dimensional but it will really be 2-D. Shading in gray and black creates a perspective and a shadow like a real frame."

"Angèle, you are too much. I've never done anything like this before."

OPPOSITE: MY FAUX LOUIS XV MIRROR

"Just pretend you are gilding a frame for the Louisiana State Museum. It's no different. It's just painted on the wall," I told her.

Lydia, my friend from Birmingham, Alabama, was coming to visit me. I decided to give her a dinner party to celebrate her stay and my new mirror. When the guests arrived and sat down at the dining table, in unison, and before noticing the gorgeous crabmeat appetizer I'd slaved over, they said, "Oh, that is the most fabulous Louis XV mirror on the wall. It looks like . . . "

I interrupted, "It's faux. My mother offered me anything from her house and when I asked her for the Louis XV mirror, she rejected my request and told me to choose something else. *So now I've fixed her and my wall.*"

There is no way that the real Louis XV mirror would have ever garnered as much attention and amusement as my faux mirror. Plus, the supplies and labor were only $300. My mother offered to pay for it. I told her not to bother. I'd be back.

So, heaven forbid that a dinner conversation should ever get dull, but if it does, I just look at myself in the faux mirror and smile. *Almost every family ends up having to divide the big brown furniture*, I tell my guests. *Even if there's only one piece.*

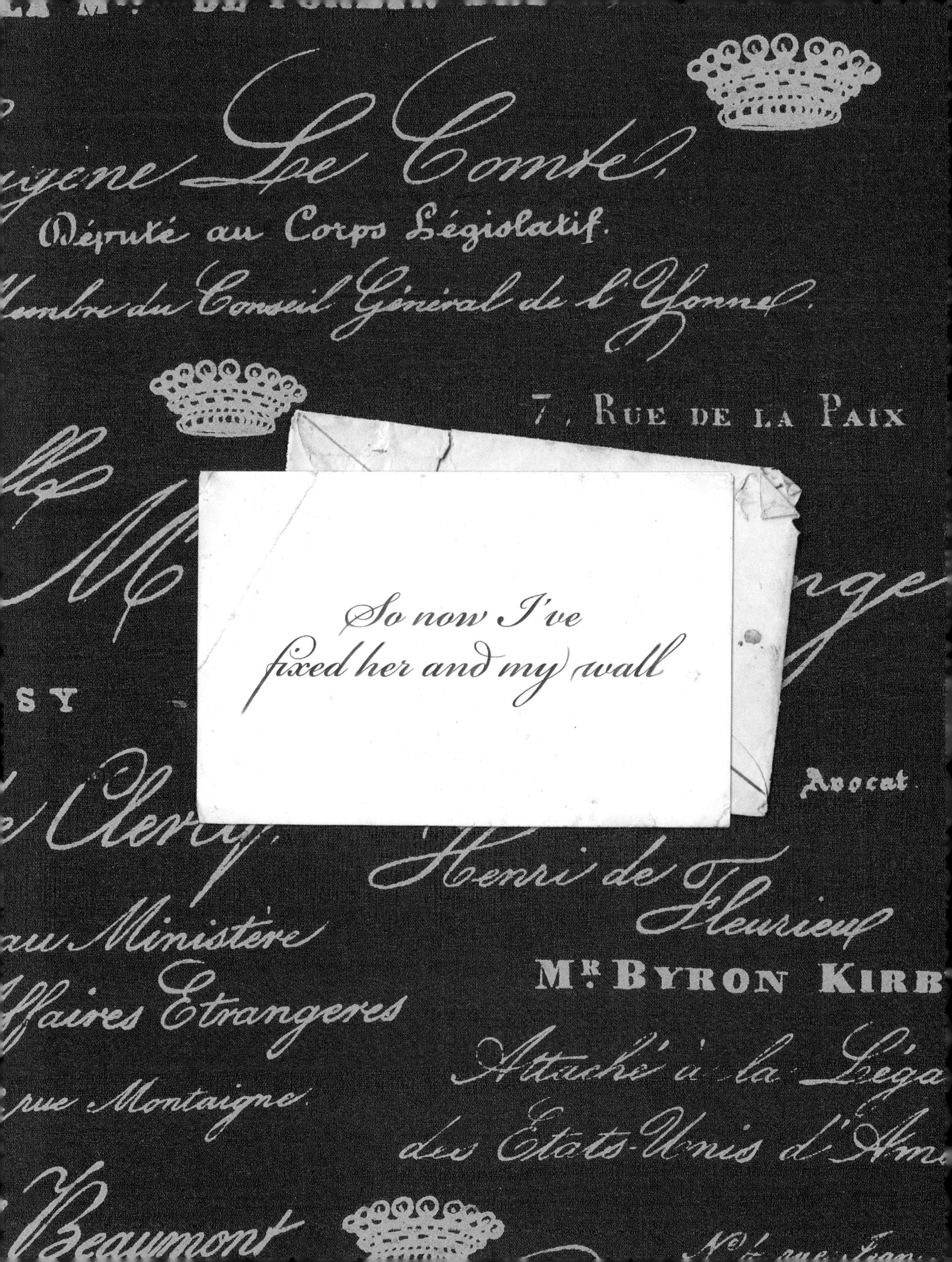
So now I've
fixed her and my wall

Recipe For
"A Conversation Piece"

RULER, COMPOSITION GOLD LEAF, SIZING—A GLUE-LIKE LIQUID FOR
ADHERING GOLD LEAF, BUTTER KNIFE OR PAINT SCRAPER

1. Take a photograph of the mirror you would like to replicate or cut out a picture of a mirror you like from a magazine, or photocopy an image from a historic or interior design book (if you don't have any, public or school libraries are a good source).

2. Decide on a size for your mirror and enlarge your photograph or picture accordingly. An architectural blueprinting company can easily enlarge the picture to your specifications.

3. Trace the mirror-frame on the wall using a ruler. Mine is a Louis XV–style frame with scrolls at the top and beading (gold-leafed circles outlined in

black) running vertically along all sides of the frame. Plain or simple lines work well, too—whatever style you prefer.

4. Buy composition gold leaf from a hobby shop, Home Depot, or Wal-Mart. The gold leaf comes in a book with individual sheets sized 5 1/2 inches by 5 1/2 inches. You will have to determine the number of sheets needed for the frame's measurements. Twenty-four carat gold leaf can also be used, but it is much more expensive and not necessary unless you want to ensure that the gold leaf will not tarnish. I personally like the patina that composition gold leaf produces.

5. Brush or spray sizing within the mirror-frame outline. Apply the sizing in small sections, then use a butter knife or paint scraper to adhere the gold leaf sheets to the wall. Apply one section at a time so that the sizing does not dry before you can cover the next section with gold leaf. More detailed instructions for application are provided on the back of the gold leaf package.

6. Measure out the size of the mirror to be placed in the frame. Call a glass or mirror company to order your desired mirror. This process should not take long and should cost about seventy-five dollars or less. The company will deliver and install the mirror on your wall within the frame outline.

7. Once the faux mirror is in place, look at yourself, smile, and remember: Almost every family ends up having to divide the big brown furniture, even if there's only one piece.

Tip

In order to make a new mirror look old, ask the glass or mirror outlet to put acid on the mirror. This is a simple process, but definitely **D.D.I.Y.**

THE BMW CABINET

Clarence Lorio's shop is located at an old grocery store in Lakeland, Louisiana. In fact, a faded sign still hangs above the screen door that reads, "Lakeview Groceries 70752." The Lakeland community is named for the oxbow lake, False River, which meanders through it. La Fausse Rivière, as it was named when Bienville discovered it, was originally a bend in the Mississippi River until the river changed its course in 1699, leaving behind a twelve-mile-long, horsehoe-shaped lake. Besides the post office and the Alma Plantation Sugar Cane Mill, Clarence's shop is the only commercial establishment in the settlement. The sugarcane fields in the 70752 zip code are some of the prettiest and most productive in the state. His shop looks like it belongs on Royal Street in New Orleans—not in the middle of a sugarcane field.

Clarence is about six-foot-three and maybe 50 years old with a full head of blond hair and lovely blue eyes. He always wears a faded pastel Lacoste shirt with khakis or white trousers and Wallabies. Unlike the former owner, Mr. Edwin David, Clarence doesn't sell groceries or act as the postmaster. The store is now an antique shop offering a mixed bag of items—some good, some okay, and some you don't want to guess where they came from.

⚜ ⚜ ⚜

One blustery, rainy Friday, I stopped in to see what Clarence had to offer. I lighted on one of those "I think I know where it came from" pieces. The object looked like it was a medical cabinet from the 1950s—not usually my thing—and was painted in a celadon green with ivory facings accented with rusty aluminum handles and pulls. Somehow it caught me. I asked Clarence if he knew anything about it,

87

and he, too, thought that it was a dental or pharmaceutical cabinet. The history really didn't matter to me; I just liked its style. I purchased the cabinet for two hundred and fifty dollars and had it delivered to New Orleans the next day for an extra twenty-five dollars.

Once I got it home, the cabinet's paint job didn't look as good as it did in Clarence's shop. I called around to inquire how one could repaint a metal cabinet. A friend of mine suggested that I take it to an auto paint shop. I phoned all around, but no auto paint shops were open on Saturday except for one that exclusively painted Corvettes.

My friend Evan offered to move the cabinet for me in his old cargo truck. The piece was about 2 feet longer than the available space, so I rode with it on the tailgate and held up an orange pennant every time we stopped for a red light. It reminded me of a favorite childhood memory—riding on the tailgate of my father's truck to feed his cattle.

Victor's Vettes was located in a strip mall on Clearview Parkway, about three miles from the New Orleans city limits. It was sandwiched between two businesses, Hubcap Heaven and Hooter's. The owner walked out of the painting garage to meet us and I immediately noticed that he had one blue glass eye. His remaining good eye wandered toward Hooter's as I made my request—two Hooter's dancers clocking in to work were obviously much more interesting than my invitation.

"Excuse me, Sir, could you have a look at the metal cabinet in my truck? I'd like to see if you can match the paint colors," I said to him. He followed me to the truck, his head still craning at the movement in the Hooter's parking lot. He tripped as he glanced back toward Evan, me, and our subject. Peering over the back of the truck, he said, "That looks like my papa's old dentist cabinet. What do you want me to do to it again?"

"Could you match this original paint color?" I asked again.

He glanced back at the women at Hooter's, and then back at me, mumbling, "Well, Miss, I only have Corvette colors—red, yellow, white, or black. Take your pick." I could not imagine the cabinet

in any of those colors, so I borrowed his phone book and located a BMW auto paint store next to the Clearview Mall, only about a mile away from the Corvette shop. Surely they would have a celadon color.

When I arrived, the owners, Mr. Ricky and his sister Miss Carla, met me outside the shop's roll-up aluminum door. Mr. Ricky wore a Sansibel blue jumpsuit with gold paint splattered all over it. Sister Carla wore cuffed jeans with a white Hanes Esplanade T-shirt. She held a live bunny rabbit under her arm. "What a cute bunny," I said.

"We go through one of these a week," she said, looking down at the rabbit and stroking his head. A cage of pet boa constrictors rested next to the cash register.

Mr. Ricky and Miss Carla took a look at the cabinet and gave me a set of BMW paint chips. The fan of paint chip colors was almost identical to my graphic design PMS (Pantone Matching System) colors. Leafing through it, I found the exact shades of the cabinets' celadon and ivory colors.

Mr. Ricky and Miss Carla had never painted a piece of furniture before but agreed to give it a try. They giggled, thinking I couldn't see them. I am certain they thought it was a ridiculous request.

⚜ ⚜ ⚜

I went back to see the results about four days later. The cabinet had been transformed; Mr. Ricky and Miss Carla beamed as proud as my niece in her patent leather Easter shoes. The piece looked as fine as a new BMW without the wheels.

I brought the cabinet to my office, but my desk and filing cabinet looked so shabby next to the freshly painted cabinet that I packed them up right away and made another trek to Mr. Ricky's.

Today I have a suite of metal furniture freshly painted in celadon green. The metal cabinet looked so chic that I promoted it to my sunroom—it is parked right next to a gilded Louis XV chair. The Corvette colors didn't work for me, but I prefer BMWs anyway.

Tip

CAR PAINT VENDORS CAN PAINT A LOT OF THINGS OTHER THAN CARS. A FRIEND OF MINE TOOK HER FRONT DOOR TO A JAGUAR DEALERSHIP IN ORDER TO ATTAIN THE HIGH-GLOSS AUBERGINE FINISH USED ON PARISIANS' FRONT DOORS.

WINTER AND SUMMER

In New Orleans, then and now, people dress their houses and themselves for summer with white canvas slipcovers and white linen suits. Come Labor Day, the heat may still be on, but poplin and linen are replaced with fall and winter fabrics in anticipation of cooler temperatures. Following that tradition, my wicker sofa was dressed up for winter with a fresh coat of paint and a new cushion in chartreuse silk. Alternatively, my recamier prepared for the out of doors by taking off its warm velvet wrap and donning a breezy pink slip. So don't discard that old sofa, give it a new dress instead.

CREOLE EXPRESSION: *When she really likes someone, my mother says, "I could winter or summer with you."*

OPPOSITE PAGE: HERE I AM WITH MY COUSIN, SARAH BRANDON SMART, ON THE OLD WICKER SOFA REUPHOLSTERED FOR A LIGHT, SUMMERY LOOK IN MY LE NOUVEAU JARDINIER FABRIC DESIGN

FOR A DARKER LOOK, I REUPHOLSTERED THE CUSHION IN CHARTREUSE SILK DUPIONI PIPED IN DARK-GREEN VELVET.

FOR WINTER, I COVERED MY RECAMIER IN DARK, RICH VELVET.

HERE IT IS RE-OUTFITTED FOR A LIGHTER FEEL IN PINK LINEN PIPED WITH WOOL HARRIS TWEED.

Cops and Robbers

❧ ❦

With twirling blue-and-red sirens blaring, a police car screeched to a halt at the corner of State and Constance Streets in uptown New Orleans. At 5:00 A.M., it was pitch black outside except for the car's headlights and oversized search lights. The policeman got out and grabbed a man holding a lampshade and table. "Drop that and put your hands up," the policeman shouted. Suddenly, all the lights turned on in the neighboring houses and the homeowners started peering out their windows to catch a glimpse of the crime.

"But Officer," Phil said, "I'm just moving things for the girls' garage sale. Really. And my two cousins are inside hauling the rest."

Courtney, my friend and co-garage-sale host, and I rushed out of the house to confirm Phil's plea with the policeman. The policeman let Phil go but warned us that we were not allowed to move anything at night according to a city ordinance. "Officer, we're just preparing for a garage sale," we said.

"Wait 'til daylight to move the rest," the policeman replied as he got back in his car.

With that, he turned his sirens off and sped away. It was the first of my garage sales—and my first unarmed robbery attempt.

⚜ ⚜ ⚜

At this garage sale, I never got out of my pajamas. When it began at 8:00 A.M., all of the merchandise was still inside rather than out on the front lawn. Anybody who has shopped at, or organized, a garage sale knows that you have to be on time or else the natives get restless. I was still figuring out prices at 8:15 A.M., when I heard a crash out front. "Hey, you idiot, I got here first, this is my parking place!

97

You just hit my car!" somebody yelled. There wasn't even anything to buy—yet. The cops were back. But for a legitimate fender-bender this time.

My front yard is about the size of two parking places. On the day of the garage sale, it was packed like the Superdome on the day of a Saints game. There was a line around the block. My neighbors were also out front ogling the scene—I had forgotten to warn them.

My friend Will helped with sales. He was so busy that he didn't have time to use the cigar box bank I provided, instead organizing all the cash and change in his sweaty shirt pocket. He later told me that he thought the money was safer on his body.

People always tell you not to bother selling clothes at garage sales; nobody will buy them. But I had proved this statement incorrect in the past. I set up a mannequin with my white Gucci pants (too tight in the waist), black halter top, and Chanel flower pin to lure buyers to the clothes rack.

One long-legged girl with enormous fake boobs (I know them when I see them) tried squeezing into one of my tops. Evan, a volunteer helper, said, "Here let me help you, I haven't done this in a long time."

With that she held her hands up and replied, "Well, I haven't had this done to me in a while." She bought that outfit and almost all the clothes on the rack.

Another friend, David, was in charge of pricing fashion items. When I walked into the room where he was sorting out clothes, I saw a red teddy and matching thong on a chair for my review. He thought he had me, but I quickly replied that I had bought that teddy set at Wal-Mart for the "Sweetarts" Valentine Ball. "I promise it's a costume," I blushed.

"Uh huh, I'm marking this 'Angèle's lingerie, collector's item, price upon request.' And I'm keeping the money. Here's your Visa card, too. I found it in the Gucci pants."

It's best to do your own pricing unless you're willing to take the fifth.

By 9:00 A.M., everything was gone except for the teddy and some Magnalite skillets. And by 10:00 A.M., I had counted the money and was figuring out how to spend it.

⚜ ⚜ ⚜

Last week, I went over to my cousin's house.

"Do you see those bookends?" she asked me with a sheepish grin.

"Yes. You got those at my garage sale."

"I did, and my sister told me that we gave those to you one Christmas."

"Well, I always give gifts that I would like to have myself. I bet you didn't get yourself a pair, now you have one." I winked at her.

Besides the good old-fashioned entertainment they provide, garage sales give me the impetus to get rid of the old before making room for the new. To see those Gucci pants of mine (minus the Visa) have another fashion season with a much more endowed owner was heartwarming. I have my own endowment—not size double D—but in the cup that runneth over. After all, one person's trash is another's treasure. I started my first pillow collection with someone's trash—velvet, silk remnants, and passementerie (trim and fringe) found at, coincidentally, a tag sale at the opposite corner of the unarmed robbery attempt. Using these bits and pieces, I created a handmade looped-gold trim with bronze doré baubles. Since the antique baubles were hard to find, I decided to use other classical motifs like crowns, fleur-de-lis, and wreaths available through brass stamping companies. All of the cushions were fabricated in jewel-tone silk taffeta, which gave them a regal feel. I named them "The Medici Collection." Each pillow was named for a Medici family member, such as "Caterina." Once I had a big enough collection in different colors and designs, I peddled them to Bergdorf Goodman, Barney's, ABC Carpet and Home, Saks Fifth Avenue, and other high-style boutiques across the country. I even learned how to set up a booth in the Jacob Javits Center in New York City, an undertaking that I wouldn't wish on anybody. Nevertheless, having a booth at a gift show does make life easier than riding the M2 bus all over town toting pillows, which is what I used to do.

My final advice is: remember your buyers could be your cousins, friends, or mother. So either offer them a steep discount if they stumble across the bookends that they gave you, or plan on explaining where the bookends came from.

Tip

OFTENTIMES, ROADKILL, LIKE MY OTTOMAN AND PLANT-STANDS-CUM-COCKTAIL TABLES, OR OTHER PIECES FOUND AT GARAGE SALES, HAVE GREAT FLAIR AND JUST NEED A LITTLE TLC. IT WOULD COST AN ARM AND A LEG TO RE-CREATE THESE PIECES, BUT WITH A LITTLE INGENUITY, THEY CAN TURN FROM RAGS TO RICHES.

Part Three
CREOLE THRIFT

MIE AS A YOUNG WOMAN

Mie was my Creole grandmother who lived with us at Parlange. Her Creole blood meant that she was a descendant of the first settlers of New Orleans, who were both French and Spanish. Mie taught me about Creole Thrift—what would later become the cornerstone of my philosophy on fashion and design. Southerners know how to get a deal without sacrificing quality for something second rate. Although forever on a budget, I, too, prefer premium brands, and the real warrior comes out in me when I've less than plenty in my pocket. That's when my most creative and resourceful ideas manifest themselves; even the cat's coat looks like more than one pelt.

You don't have to be a Creole to adhere to Creole Thrift philosophy; just don't consider a hiccup in a project to be a failure, but rather an opportunity for something else to grow out of your original intent. Scarlett in *Gone with the Wind* ripped down those velvet curtains to make herself a beautiful hat and gown; it didn't change her temper, but it did bring back her glamour. Being inventive, resourceful, creative, and building on pieces that you already have can make for amazing end results and a clever outcome.

CREOLE THRIFT

✦✦ ✦✦

Pouring drugstore bourbon into an empty bottle of Jack Daniels is not Creole Thrift. Our very rich friends, who pretended to be Creoles, used to do this little trick; I caught them one time, pouring K & B (a legendary New Orleans drugstore now out of business) bourbon into a Jack Daniels bottle. That's Cheap (and tacky), not Creole Thrift—Creoles like premium brands. My grandmother Mie used to make cocktail dresses for herself from her old draperies. For my parents' wedding, she

salvaged the damask and fringe of some threadbare and faded silk swags to embellish the bodice on her mother-of-the-groom gown. In my parents' wedding album, Mie and her dress look ravishing. Being thrifty begets some of the most inspiring creations.

Though there are a variety of interpretations of the term "Creole," the most appropriate definition in this instance is referenced in *The Oxford Concise Dictionary* as "a white descendent of French settlers in the Southern United States." French Creoles' interests and manner were influenced by Paris rather than New York or Washington, and their culture was one of geniality and cosmopolitanism. They established the French Quarter of New Orleans.

MIE AND POPS AT MY PARENTS' WEDDING

OPPOSITE: FROM *HOLIDAY* MAGAZINE, MARCH 1952; FROM LEFT TO RIGHT: POPS, MIE, A VISITING STUDENT, AND MY FATHER

105

GOVERNOR MURPHY J. FOSTER, GOVERNOR MCCUERY,
LT. GOVERNOR CHARLES PARLANGE

POPS AS A YOUNG MAN

THE "OVAL SALON"

Mie was proud of her Creole heritage, as all Creoles are likely to be, but what she was really proud of was her "Creole Thrift." My guess is that Creole Thrift became a necessity, not only after the Civil War, but also subsequently during the Depression and other hard times. Even when in the black, however, a Creole doesn't just throw money around as a parvenu would. Although they like quality and first-class trappings, Creoles intuitively know there are ways to be resourceful; to make do or reinvent what you have on hand.

Mie imbued me with Creole Thrift.

My tennis partner gets the Sunday *New York Times*. On the Tuesday afterwards, she drops the paper off at my house. I probably wouldn't have time to read it anyway on Sunday, so I save myself five dollars and get it hand-delivered. I do sometimes miss having the paper to read with my Community dark roast coffee on Sunday after a late Saturday night. But that's Creole Thrift.

MY FATHER

Don't think that being cheap and having Creole Thrift mean the same thing, although sometimes they overlap. A Creole would spend any amount of money on good wine, education, books, the opera (the first opera in America was held in New Orleans), and other things related to culture, status, and good living. Why, some people even mortgage their homes just so their daughter can be Queen of Rex or Comus—the latter being the oldest and most exclusive Mardi Gras organization and ball. But as ridiculous, outrageous, and provincial as this may seem, these people know something that others don't: It's résumé-building. Establishing contacts and friendships that take you through life is actually a very broad-minded plan of action. Still, it's a weak case for Creole Thrift when one goes into debt for a fantasy crown. There's a lot more to life than wearing a tiara for six hours of New Orleans fame.

A good friend of mine was queen of Carnival. Although her mother is from the Midwest and wasn't a Creole, now that my friend is of age, she and her entire family are enrolled in my Creole

Thrift Vocational School. That's a nonpublished number and address. Her beautiful rhinestone-studded dress and train had been recycled five times before she wore it on Carnival night. She, like Mie, embellished her preowned dress with some shiny Swarovski crystals transforming it into a one-of-a-kind knockout gown.

Now that's Creole Thrift. And she used the money she saved to pay for her junior year abroad.

That's exactly what a Creole would do.

Mie died at the age of 92, while I was in the midst of taking final exams. When I finally got to the hospital, I didn't know she had already died. The nurse told me that the last thing Mie said to her was,

"That's a right nice design on the curtains in this dismal hospital room. If I had my sewing machine with me, I'd get you to take them down and I'd make myself a receiving jacket out of the fabric."

"You'd probably get kicked out of The Lady of the Lake Hospital for that Miss Paule," the nurse said, laughing.

"O Mon Dieu," *O My God*, which was a favorite expression of hers.

As much as I wanted to cry instead of laugh, I couldn't help myself. Till the bitter end, Mie was working her Creole Thrift. She probably would have liked "Creole Thrift" on her tombstone, had it not cost an extra line.

CREOLE EXPRESSION:

"The woods are full of them." Mie said this when she referred to big families.

SIX GENERATIONS HAVE LIVED IN THIS OLD LOUISIANA HOME

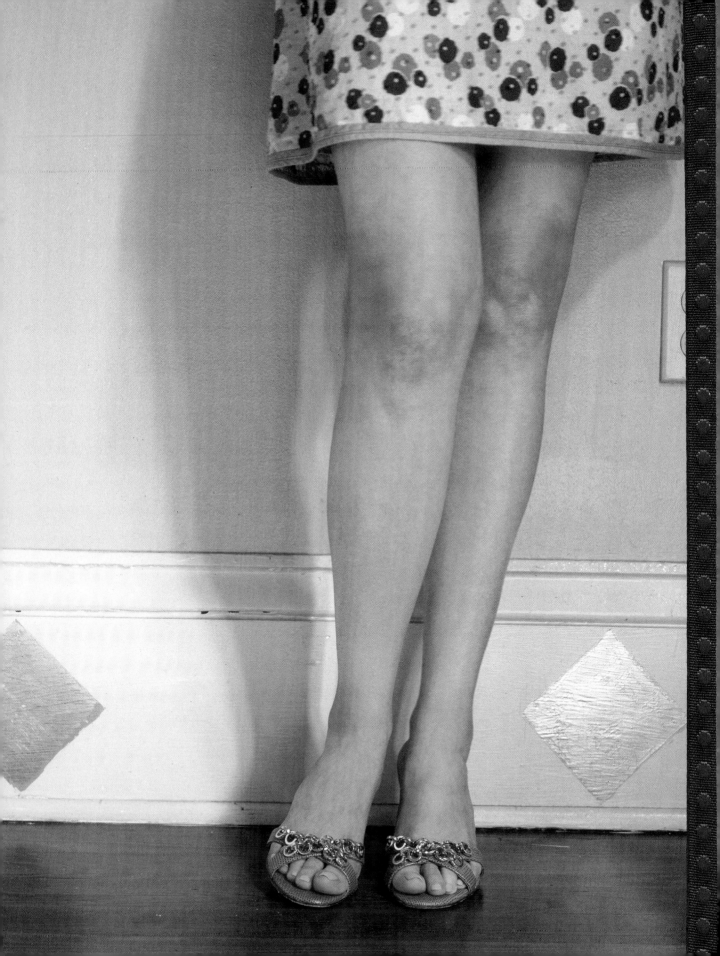

THE MIDAS TOUCH

✦

One day Mr. Yune David made an appointment to see my father about his leg. Daddy was the president of Pointe Coupée Parish and handled all sorts of requests from his constituents. "Mr. Walter, I need you to see if you can get me a new leg from Congressman Jimmy Morrison," he said, hobbling into my father's office. Mr. Yune had been wounded in World War II and had a wooden leg.

"Now Yune, what's wrong with the prosthetic leg you have?" Daddy asked him.

"It got eaten up by termites. I took it off when I was laid up with pneumonia and put it in the corner of the room. Next thing I knew, it was filled up with those terrible bugs."

My father called the congressman and explained Yune's situation. Yune had a new leg within a week, thanks to everyone's concern.

Termites are a burden in New Orleans, too, and can cripple a house just as easily as it crippled Mr. Yune's wooden leg. A few years back, the Terminix representative came for his annual inspection and found small pin-like holes in my living room's baseboards. Although my house was definitely a termite victim, the inspector said that I could defer the treatment for a while. Fumigating for wood termites is a big expense, and since my house was not a candidate for a congressman's pity, the financial responsibility was on my nickel.

Even though the holes were pin-size, they were noticeable. Fine shavings oozed out from the baseboards where the termites worked. Since I would be receiving professional termite treatment within a year, I tried to think of a cosmetic solution in the meantime. Painting would cost a fortune and was a waste of money. But another idea soon came to me as I noticed the number of gold-leafed furniture pieces and frames in my living room. Square sheets of gold leaf could be turned 45° to create a diamond shape that would cover up the holes along the baseboards. The same design and execution could be performed on the molding to complement the baseboards.

Teenie, my gold-leaf expert, performed the job. She spaced out the 5-inch-by-5-inch gold leaf squares all along the living room's baseboard. The gold diamonds were placed 16 inches apart. Next, she cut the gold-leaf squares to a 2-inch-by-2-inch size for the narrow molding. These smaller diamonds were spaced 16 inches apart from each other, as well. The job took a day and a half to complete and was far less expensive and time-consuming than a new paint job. The furniture sparkled against the new backdrop; now the eye was drawn to the harlequin design rather than the holes. I prayed the termites wouldn't have the Midas touch.

My father didn't think of this cosmetic remedy for Mr. Yune's bad leg. But then again, Mr. Yune had no intention of showing it off. I, on the other hand, *did* want to show off my room, even if there were termites masked behind the harlequins.

Although my house has now been fumigated, the gold harlequins remain. I didn't want to miss the chance to brag: *My living room is encased in diamonds, gold, and dead bodies.*

Recipe For
"The Midas Touch"

Ingredients

RULER, COMPOSITION OR IMITATION GOLD LEAF, 24-KARAT GOLD LEAF,

OR SILVER LEAF, 2 FLUID OUNCES SIZING

1. Measure out in equidistance where you want to place the gold-leaf harlequins on your floor and ceiling molding. Trace a 5 1/2-by-5 1/2-inch space for each harlequin using a pencil. Determine how many leaves you will need to cover each space and buy the number of gold-leaf books necessary. There are approximately 25 leaves per book.

2. Brush sizing onto one of the 5 1/2-by-5 1/2-inch spaces and quickly adhere the gold leaf to the area before the sizing dries. Repeat this procedure, covering the remaining spaces with gold leaves. Both the sizing and the gold-leaf book should include more advanced instructions for leafing.

WALL FLOWERS

⟶✳ ❦⟵

Let me tell you about the beginning of my sea-foam room. There's no sea, no foam, just the muddy Mississippi a few blocks down the street. But I'm a great pretender.

Ann Koerner is the proprietress of Ann Koerner Antiques on Magazine Street in New Orleans. She has three rooms in a shotgun house where she artfully displays her wares. I can always find something at Ann's, which is just what happened one day when I stumbled in there without a plan. Life's what happens when you're *not* making other plans.

My house was being photographed for an interiors magazine, and since my sunroom had been featured before in another magazine, I had to change it on my very small budget. I was a little tired of it anyway: the curtains were burlap-bare and my white canvas sofa was becoming beige. I'm afraid of beige.

Browsing through Ann's, I really didn't have anything particular in mind when suddenly I found a pile of twenty or so old prints. Each watercolor print was a unique stylized flower or fern with an Asian flair painted on either a celadon or robin's egg–colored paper. "Oh, Ann," I gasped, "what are these gorgeous aqua and black designs?"

"Those are old wallpaper designs and I'd sell them to you for twenty dollars each," she said, surprised at my interest.

"Twenty dollars each? What's so special about them? Would you take fifteen dollars each if I bought the whole lot?"

What Ann didn't know was that before I had negotiated the price, I had already figured out the end result. I would frame each design in black stock frames (available at Home Depot, Target, or Bed Bath and Beyond), and mass them on the wall as the centerpiece to my room.

Ann accepted my offer.

Now that I had a theme, I had to coordinate the rest of the room. I replaced my wicker sofa with a fifty-dollar version from The Salvation Army. Next, I ordered pale-aqua-colored linen for the sofa and blue-green linen for the piping to make a slipcover. Beverly Beavers, a talented slipcover-maker, bumped my order ahead since she knew I had an urgent deadline. Although there are plenty of good slip-coverers in New Orleans, I always anticipate the installation of Beverly's work. She is the only person I allow to smoke in my house, and because I let her smoke, she confesses all of her goings-on at the Cat's Meow in the French Quarter. The Cat's Meow has karaoke, and with a cigarette and a hangover, Beverly repeats her Cat's Meow performance for me live and in person. Satisfaction is guaranteed with Beverly's slipcover and entertainment.

Everything started to fall into place for my new sunroom. I painted the walls a Pratt and Lambert paint color called "Bay." The room immediately took on a cool and restful atmosphere. Continuing with the sea-foam theme, I picked out a painted French bistro table with an aqua top and pale yellow legs. Several years ago, my brother loaned me his prized zebra skin. I parked it in my living room and just never had a chance to return it to him—squatter's rights. The zebra found a new grazing pasture in the sunroom where it pulled together the black-framed wallpaper designs.

My "A Cameo Appearance" (page 119) coffee table, formerly at my French Quarter apartment, was just the right shade of algae to mix with the sofa, and the "Everybody Looks Good in Sepia Tones" (page 49) photo-curtains balanced the room with a sense of history. When I surveyed my completed sunroom, I felt like the real wallflower. So many strong, amusing personalities stood out, and although they were not in the same company as before, the pieces socialized well together. It's sort of like the makings of a good party. No one may know each other before the party, but they 0all find something in common by the end.

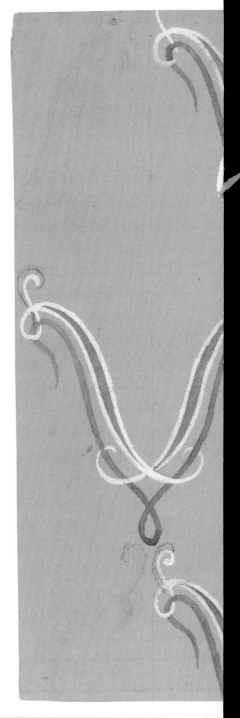

A CAMEO APPEARANCE

✦ ✦ ✦

"It's all the same nightmare people you see in New York," a journalist friend told me. "Why would you ever consider such an invitation?" But I wasn't going to see those people. A dear friend invited me to his house in Bridgehampton to see the ocean, relax, and have a look around. Plus, I had heard there were some great tag sales!

Mish and I took the Jitney, a luxury bus, out to the Hamptons. The Bridgehampton stop was adjacent to an old-fashioned ice cream parlor. With our two chocolate-dipped hard cones, we walked to Mish's house, a charming shingled cottage about 500 yards from the main street. Mish dropped his duffel at the front door, turned on the lights in the original 1940s kitchen, and then escorted me to the guest room—a cubbyhole so small that only a twin bed fit inside. The bed was made up with the most beautiful, old-fashioned cotton sheets (purchased at a local tag sale), which were monogrammed on the border with a slightly tattered "A". There was nothing nightmarish about the Hamptons to me.

⚜ ⚜ ⚜

With no plans for the next day, Mish suggested that we go to the marvelous tag sales in nearby Sag Harbor. The best finds were discovered early in the morning. Afterwards, we could ride bikes to the beach.

En route to Sag Harbor, Mish and I saw family-run vegetable stands with gorgeous Silver Queen corn, tomatoes, arugula, and potatoes. I had no idea this was such an agricultural area and kept remarking on the beauty and unpretentiousness of our surroundings. That was until I saw the hedges, and what was behind those hedges: very big shingled houses. Although their size was grand, there was something very warm and cozy about these houses behind hedges. Perhaps it was the landscaping. Although well kept, the gardens didn't have a formal feeling, but rather a thoughtful, unmanicured nature. Next stop was the Maidstone Club, then more hedges and big, big houses. We proceeded past these hedges to Sag Harbor and Sage Street Antiques, where the premier tag sale is located. Very well-dressed-trying-to-look-badly-dressed (wrinkled clothes, that's all) men and women had lined up, reading the *New York Times* and *Hamptons Magazine* while waiting for Sage Street to open its doors.

Once we got past the old televisions and radios, I proceeded to the least-interesting-looking room. That's what I always do to steer away from the crowd. Whereas the entrance rooms were decorated with displays of merchandise, this room just seemed to have a bunch of stuff left over from a long day of setting up. In this quiet room I found wonderful lamps, nearly new dishes, and hotel silver—all at amazing bargains. I couldn't believe it, especially coming from New Orleans where we have amazing estate sales and auctions. New Orleans had nothing on these finds. Rummaging through a box of old books such as *Wining and Dining with Rhyme and Reason* and *The Whore's Rhetorick* (must-haves), I spotted a palm-size plaster cameo of an ancient religious figure. I picked it up and put it aside, thinking it was interesting but not knowing which saint or prophet it was. Rustling through the box, I discovered eight more of these cameos—all with different faces. Finding these other eight made the original one have much more appeal. They looked like monks, many with hoods or shawls atop their heads, and some were identified in Latin, although the writing was illegible. I really didn't care who they were, they could be pagans for all I knew, but they were mine if I could afford them. The Sage Street proprietress said they were ten dollars each and that sounded fair enough to me. With my two books and my nine men of uncertain origins, I was a very happy Hamptoneer.

Two years later, still savoring my delightful Bridgehampton visit, I needed a sturdy and stain-proof coffee table for my French Quarter apartment.

I had always wanted something made of concrete that didn't look like a driveway. An architect friend, William Sonner, told me about a place that dyed concrete. Color is always good. Immediately, I thought of my medallions. They would be perfect cast in a concrete table top, and I could have Phil, an iron worker, make a simple iron base.

Architectural Ornaments, a New Orleans company that reproduces wooden columns in plaster, had once reproduced some wooden chairs for me in plaster to cut the cost of hand-carving. Surely Beth, the owner, could copy and cast these cameos, but first I had to ask if she could set them in a concrete block. She told me that it would be a breeze.

I felt certain that ordering a concrete block involved nothing more than providing dimensions over the telephone. But I also wanted the concrete dyed, similar to the way people dye concrete to create a pale-pink driveway. In fact, the *only* dyed concrete I had ever seen was pale-pink, but I didn't want a pink coffee table. I found a company that pours concrete on South Jefferson Davis Parkway, and although they said that my project wouldn't be a problem, I would have to come over to see their selection of dyes.

The concrete company's dye colors and the Corvette paint deck were just about the same palette: primary. I had them mix together a royal blue and a sunny yellow to produce a lovely shade of green. Green would be a nice background for the men.

The table top was poured to my specifications (16 inches by 31 by 3 1/2 inches), and the shade of green was perfect. And yet, I had forgotten one thing: the weight. When I tried to pick the table up, I hadn't realized that it would weigh over 100 pounds. Thank goodness Phil hadn't made the base yet as I would have to be certain it could handle the stress of this much weight.

While Beth set the men according to my choice of rank, Phil whipped up the iron base. Both Phil and Beth made their deliveries to my French Quarter apartment. I forgot to mention to the concrete transporters that my building is very old and I'm on the top floor. Bless their hearts, I think they almost passed out getting that slab up the narrow, rickety stairwell.

"Little miss," one of the guys said, gasping for breath, "you be sure where you want this table, 'cuz you'll never be able to move this by yourself." Down they went, fitting the slab onto the iron base. They were right: that table was not moving unless it went through the second story into the landlady's parlor.

The table is not childproof, or for that matter, adult proof, and would take out anybody if you hit your head on the corner. But it serves as the best footrest (you just whisk off any dirt or mud), the

perfect rest-stop for a drink (no glass rings as concrete absorbs liquid), and an amazing conversation piece. You see, those nine men making their cameo appearances have yet to be identified, and I know some pretty smart people.

THINK OF USING UNEXPECTED MATERIALS, SUCH AS CONCRETE, PLASTER, OR EVEN RESIN FOR FABRICATING FUNCTIONAL PIECES LIKE MY CAMEO APPEARANCE COFFEE TABLE.

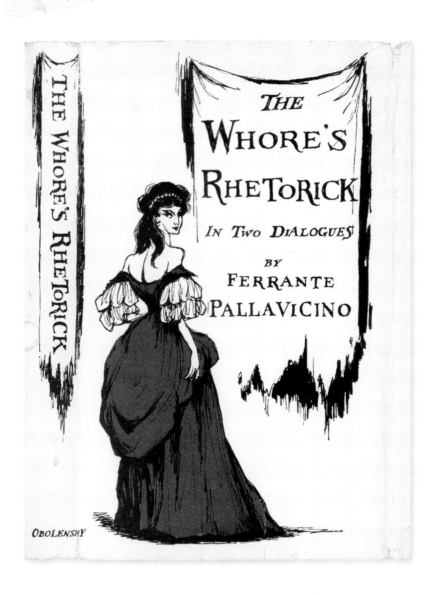

Part Four

WHIMSY AND FANTASY

Blithe spirit   *For Lucy with much love*   *Stephania Dinkins*

MY MOTHER SWINGING BAVON SHENETTE, CLAUDE, AND MONIQUE

Both whimsy and fantasy are key ingredients to the success of a hospitable and comfortable home, with a splash of irreverence thrown into the mix.

I come from a long line of storytellers who had marvelous senses of humor. Think of New Orleans as a frothy cocktail of many different cultures—Spanish, French, Caribbean, and African-American. Much of our humor comes from the wisdom and folklore of this cross section of traditions. As a result, humor is a given in my mode of operation—there are so many pieces in my house that amuse me or bring back wonderful memories. Just like a well-rounded person, a great house needs to have smarts, good looks, kindness, and foremost in my estimation, a sense of humor.

When I was a little girl, I always had a bigger plan for myself. I think this was because my great-great-grandmother had led such a glamorous life. She was a courageous woman who ran a plantation with great success in spite of being a Southern Belle. Fantasizing about her life led my brothers and me to construct little tents in the gardens at Parlange where we orchestrated everything from our famous birthday parties—no parents allowed—to creating luxurious habitats for our cats and dogs.

My brothers did the carpentry, I did the decorating. But you don't have to be a kid to create a tent. Whether it's a tent or a duck blind, you can transport yourself from the office to wherever that fun factory might be for you. There are so few surprises left in life today, I've made the unexpected a cause célèbre in my decorating method. That's why they call it make-believe.

FROM LEFT: A FRIEND, ME, AND MY COUSIN, MARTHA BRANDON

Creole Thrift

HORSEBACK RIDES
$1
KLEENEX
2 FOR A NICKEL

AN ADVERTISEMENT FOR ONE OF MY EARLY
ENTREPRENEURIAL EFFORTS. I NEVER HAD A BETTER
MARGIN ON ANY PRODUCT THAN I DID ON THE
"KLEENEX 2 FOR 5¢."

call working willy
10 ¢
Put out garbage
5 ¢
walk dog's
15 ¢
empty waste baskets
5 ¢
get the paper
25 ¢
wash car
15 ¢
raking laevs
10 ¢
ruming errands at kb
5 ¢ or 10 ¢
Pick up paper in yard

Plus any ood gobs
866-1689
618 Audubon.

A SIMILAR ADVERTISEMENT FROM ONE OF MY FRIENDS

Y.B.&y. a vee's 5¢ to
white paint spray
small black enamel (jar)
little heart things

Sonniers
Plaster of Paris

Morgan's
nailey blue a clean stockings

maybey paper cups

magrolia
fingernail polish
Mac Froger

ONE OF MY EARLY SHOPPING LISTS

UNDER THE BIG TOP

When my brothers and I were children, my mother assured us that fairies were living under the enormous live oak trees in our garden. We left notes and trinkets for the fairies and they would write us thank-you notes for their presents. We also set up small tents, not for camping, but for having little parties. Sometimes I would bring my dolls inside and have a party for them. There was something secretive and safe about being in a tent, and the best part was that adults couldn't fit in it: No trespassing.

Once I became an adult, I found myself attracted again to tents, pavilions, and theater sets. Maybe I was missing those early fantasies, but unconsciously, I started collecting circus-inspired items. I didn't even think about starting a collection; I was simply drawn to the amusing tricks and entertaining acts of circus performers, who seem so gay and happy-go-lucky. Some of my original purchases were jelly glasses with drawings of girls performing arabesques on horses and old French photograph slides once used with a handheld projector to show a clown standing on one leg: "*Équilbré.*" Another

favorite acquisition was a scarlet-colored French book illustrated with a clown walking a tightrope. All these pieces tickled me and still do. One time a friend came over and picked up on my house's whimsical feeling and playful accessories. I didn't even realize until then that I had something of a collection.

But what I didn't have was a tent. I needed a tent to cover my dining room table, to make an ordinary dinner party feel as if you were someplace else. Then no one would worry about the food.

I found examples of tents while searching through my French circus book and my collection of old postcards with beach pavilions. The combination of elements from a couple of these photos would make for a good tent. After William, an architect and a dear friend, drew the tent to scale, I took the drawing to Phil, a genius iron worker, who could make just about anything out of metal. Phil had an iron workshop across the Mississippi River from New Orleans. He had made beds and chairs for me in the past, and I felt certain that, with some convincing, he could make a tent frame.

As expected, Phil said that he had never made a tent and asked why I couldn't just buy one out of a catalog. "Now Phil, you know it couldn't be that easy," I replied, showing him the drawing. "My tent needs to look like this beautiful drawing."

Phil knew he could master the tent frame, even though he thought it was a bit ridiculous to put a tent over my dining room table. "Angèle, this job is going to take a little longer—and I might have to attend a circus to see how you put up a tent," he winked.

"But the circus has just left town and I'm having a dinner party soon," I said.

About two weeks later, Phil showed me the tent frame that his men had assembled. It looked great. Now all I had to do was pick a color for them and spray-paint it. I chose cornflower blue, a stock paint color from Freret Hardware, which is an old-fashioned New Orleans store.

The next task was to cover the tent with fabric. After my seamstress and I measured the top of the tent, she made a pattern. I alternated each section with cornflower-blue silk dupioni and silver-metallic silk organza. It took a total of about 27 yards. To finish it, my seamstress bordered the fabric with upside-down triangle points in the same cornflower-blue dupioni. Eight-millimeter gold balls that I had bought from a bead shop dangled from each triangle point.

The tent was ready to be installed over my table. Some friends helped assemble the frame and finally, we draped the tent top over it. All that was missing were some panels so that you could close yourself up in the tent if you liked.

A standard width of fabric is 45 inches. One width by 96 inches long, seamed on all sides and with nine ties on top, would make a panel. There would be two at each corner for privacy. Khanh, my seamstress, made these, as well. They were a breeze compared to the tent top.

Everything about the tent seemed magical; it made the entire room look exotic. But when I sat at the table under the tent and looked all around I noticed that something didn't seem right. Of course! There was no chandelier hanging from the middle—almost like being without a toothbrush for me.

I had a funnel-shaped chandelier from Bush Antiques in New Orleans that I hadn't done anything with yet. This would be a perfect place to hang it. My gold-leaf

expert silver-leafed the chandelier and I hung it from the tent's center pole using a very long extension cord. The tent and the table glowed.

The first tent guest was Phil, whom I had invited over for some of my dark roast Community coffee. Phil took a sip and said, "This sure beats my wife's cooking."

I wasn't sure whether he was talking about my coffee or being under the big top with me. I'd like to think that the way to a man's heart is under my tent.

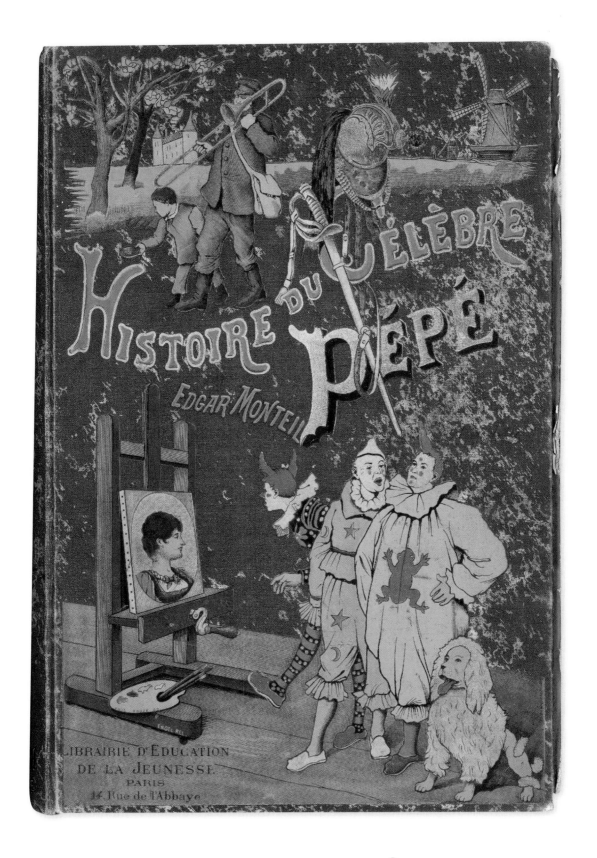

Recipe For
"Under the Big Top"

IRON (CONSULT WITH AN IRON WORKER), KRAFT PAPER, FABRIC,
3 DOZEN 18-MILLIMETER GOLD BALLS, GOLD CORDING

1. Find a picture of a tent you like.

2. Look in the yellow pages under "Iron Workers, Welders." Ask if the iron workers make custom pieces and can work from a photograph. Determine the dimensions of the square or circle dining room table that the tent will cover.

3. Using Kraft paper, make a pattern of one of the sections of the tent top.

4. Look in the yellow pages for dressmakers. The tent top will take some expertise. A good seamstress will be able to tell you the yardage needed for the entire top of the tent (about 27 yards) and for the panels, which are approximately 45 inches by 96 inches and take 3 yards each. If you want 2 panels on each

corner, you will need 12 yards for the panels. The panels hang with gold cording, which takes about 3 yards to make 9 ties per panel. The harlequin points take 5 yards. A bead shop will have gold balls available to dangle from each point. The total amount of balls needed is 33.

5. Select your fabric and gold cording at a fabric shop. Fabric is now available through the Internet, too, where you can view color swatches of dupioni and silk metallic organza before ordering. If you don't know what the actual fabric looks and feels like, I suggest first viewing it at a local fabric shop. These types of fabrics are available at most higher-end dress and interior fabric shops.

6. The iron worker will deliver the tent to your house. Make sure that the iron worker is there to instruct the initial installation should you want to take the frame down. You will need 2 or 3 people to help assemble the tent.

7. Once the tent is erected, drape the fabric tent top over the top of the frame. The tent top should fit like a loose slip cover. Hang two panels at each corner for privacy or just for effect.

Sometimes it only takes one little item to spark your imagination. Here are more examples of circus-themed projects that were inspired by my antique glass slide of illustrated acrobatics.

THE INSPIRATION: MY ANTIQUE ACROBATICS GLASS SLIDE

OPPOSITE: GRETCHEN HOWARD, A DECORATIVE PAINTER, ENLARGED AND PAINTED THE LE NAGEUR (THE SWIMMER) AND LES PANTOUFFLES (THE PANTALOONS) IMAGES ON A MURAL FOR MY FRIEND'S SON, PETER LAUGHLIN.

AN EMBROIDERED ACROBATIC COVERLET

LE NAGEUR

L'ÉQUILIBRE

LES PANTOUFFLES

L'ÉCHELLE

LES ÉCHASSES

LES BOUTEILLES

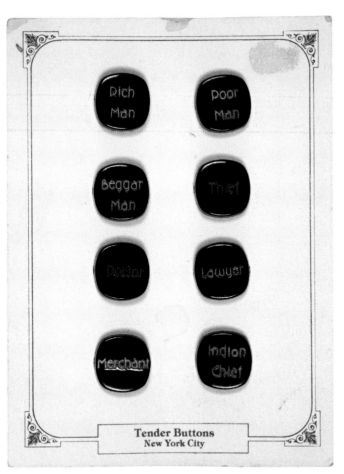

I FOUND THESE AT A BUTTON STORE AND JUST ADORED THEM.
LATER THEY INSPIRED ME TO ILLUSTRATE AND PRODUCE A
COLLECTION OF COCKTAIL NAPKINS.

RICHMAN

POORMAN

THIEF

LAWYER

ERCHANT

INDIAN CHIEF

EMBROIDERED COCKTAIL NAPKINS

PECANS ON FIRE
(FROM PAMELA HUBBELL
OF BATON ROUGE, LOUISIANA)

1 ¹/₂ teaspoons salt
1 ¹/₂ teaspoons freshly ground black pepper
1 ¹/₂ teaspoons cayenne pepper
2 ¹/₄ teaspoons sweet paprika
1 pound extra-large pecan halves
1 cup confectioners' sugar
1 quart canola oil

1. Mix the salt, black pepper, cayenne pepper, and paprika in a large bowl. Blanch the pecans in boiling water for 5 minutes, then drain well. Coat the nuts with the confectioners' sugar.

2. Heat the oil in a large pot over moderately high heat. Add the pecans and fry until golden brown, about 4 minutes. With a slotted spoon, transfer the pecans to the seasoning mixture and toss until well coated. Let cool completely before serving.

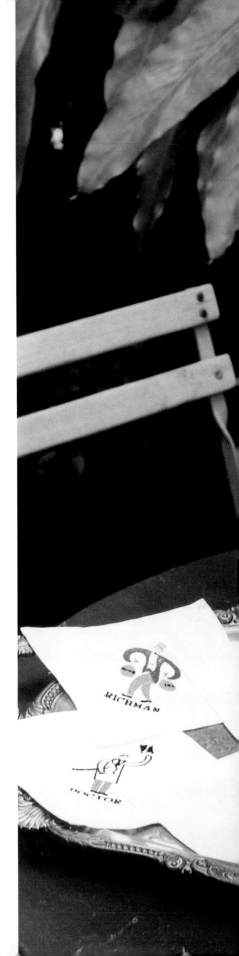

SAZERAC (FROM THE SAZERAC BAR IN NEW ORLEANS WHERE IT WAS INVENTED)

Crushed ice

1 teaspoon absinthe, Pernod, or Herbsaint Liqueur

1 teaspoon sugar, 1 sugar cube, or 1 teaspoon simple syrup

1 jigger, or 1 1/2 ounces, rye whiskey (I prefer Jack Daniels Rye whiskey)

3 dashes Peychaud's bitters

1 lemon peel twist

1. Chill an old-fashioned glass by filling it with crushed ice or refrigerating it for at least 30 minutes.

2. In a separate glass, add the Herbsaint, absinthe, or Pernod; swirl it around to coat the entire sides and the bottom of the glass. Discard the excess.

3. In a cocktail shaker, add the sugar, rye whiskey, bitters, and four or five small ice cubes. Shake gently for about 30 seconds; strain into the prepared old-fashioned glass. Twist lemon peel over the drink and then place in the drink.

Yield: 1 serving.

ICE COFFEE

(NEW ORLEANS—STYLE, COLD WATER DRIP AND DIFFERENT FROM ANY OTHER RECIPE IN THE COUNTRY—TOUCHÉ!)

For this recipe, I recommend using the Toddy Cold Brew Coffee System supplied by PJ's Coffee Shop in New Orleans.

1 pound PJ's Viennese coffee, or any other coarsely ground coffee
Splash pure vanilla extract

1. Pour 2 cups of water into the bottom of the Toddy brewing container, then add 1/2 pound of the coffee.
2. Pour 5 cups of water slowly and in circular motion over the grounds. Add the remaining 1/2 pound of coffee.
3. Wait 5 minutes, then slowly add 2 cups of water. Do not stir the grounds. Lightly tap the top layer of grounds with the back of a spoon to ensure that all of the grounds get wet.
4. Let brew for 12 hours.
5. Remove the stopper and let the coffee concentrate flow into the glass decanter. Add the splash of pure vanilla extract to the concentrate. Refrigerate and mix with water and/or milk when ready to use. The concentrate remains fresh for up to 14 days.

Yield: 6 cups (48 ounces) of coffee concentrate.

CREOLE EXPRESSION:
"Dim the lights and keep moving."

NOT FOR THE BIRDS

❦

I love a ladybug. Always have. Ladybugs bring good luck; they're messengers of happiness. I have a pair of red sandals adorned with a ladybug on each thong. I bought them, not out of necessity, but for the ladybugs. The Ladybug Shop on Royal Street was one of my favorite shops as a teenager. I even have a friend who named her very chic shop, "Ladybug and Chocolate"; it has nothing to do with ladybugs and plenty to do with chocolate, lingerie, pretty, fluffy powder puffs, and bath products. In spring, ladybugs multiply by the thousands and there is so much luck and happiness that even the Dalai Lama can't keep up with it all. Neither can I.

Pigeonniers, in France and in early French colonial architecture, were built for raising squab, young pigeon, which was considered a delicacy. These amazing, rare buildings included built-in wooden nesting shelves for the birds as well as square openings that encircled the building so that the birds could fly in and out at will. At Parlange, there is a pair of octagonal pigeonniers which grace the front entrance to the house. They are not only lovely but also of important architectural interest; there are not many pigeonniers left from the early houses.

When I was a child, my father stored hay for his cattle on both floors of the pigeonnier. One of my favorite pastimes was jumping from the second story down to the first onto the hay bales. The jump was high, very scary, and made my stomach tingle. But after each jump, I'd climb right back up on the hay bales and do it over and over again.

⚜ ⚜ ⚜

About twenty years ago, my brother took two years off from his civil engineering firm to complete a major renovation at Parlange, restoring the entire house and the pigeonniers. Although Parlange had been preserved through the years, it needed some modern bathrooms, central air and heat, and the general maintenance that old houses need.

Brandon did a beautiful job restoring both pigeonniers, transforming one into his office, the other into a guesthouse—not for the birds. But we've always had a problem with little creatures who seek shelter in the pigeonniers. Wasps were the first intruders. We used Loropan and Bengal bombs to get rid of them but they continued to find entrances.

One time, an old boyfriend of mine was visiting me and had too much to drink. Just as I was making sure that he was all settled in the pigeonnier, he started that half-sleeping, half-awake, alcohol-influenced gibberish.

"Percy, what was that you just said?" He was already lying down on top of the twin bed in full tuxedo; scotch, soda, and cigarette on the bedside table.

"Angèle, there are generals and lieutenant governors underneath me."

"What in the world are you talking about? Those are your suspenders that you haven't taken off yet. If you want to go to sleep in full dress, that's fine, but I'd want to put on my pajamas."

Then Percy was out for the night. I tucked him and his tuxedo in, turned off the lights, and walked up to the big house to go to bed.

In the middle of the night, my mother heard someone knocking on the back door to the house. She got out of bed and apprehensively tiptoed to the door where she found Percy, who had been stung out of the pigeonnier by all those "lieutenant governors and generals," also known as wasps. My mother made a meat tenderizer paste and put it on his numerous stings. Percy was stoic, although highly allergic to wasps, and ran a fever for a few days. That was when my mother turned the corner on Percy. She decided, finally, that he was not the rogue she had thought he was. I never knew it would take wasps to get her approval. Of course, typical of me, once I got the approval, I was on to other options. But Percy and his courage will always be dear to me and my family.

The next intruders in the pigeonniers were flying squirrels. Now, although they don't sting, squirrels are much larger and don't come out until the lights are off.

INSIDE THE PIGEONNIER

My friends Mish and Robert once stayed in the pigeonnier during a visit from New York City. I had warned them that although no one had witnessed any flying squirrels recently, there was a possibility that some could still be there. It was hard for us to know since nobody stayed in the pigeonnier unless they were guests. I assured Mish and Robert that squirrels were very innocent creatures but that it was best to have a stiff drink before going to bed.

At daybreak the next morning, Brandon went out to check the cattle and noticed Robert sitting on the steps of the pigeonnier. Robert Ruffino is the creative director of Tiffany's and looks the part of a real New Yorker. Always dressed to the nines, with jet-black hair and eyes, he looks a bit severe as if nothing could bother him. Brandon hollered from the truck to him, "Everything okay, Robert? You're up mighty early."

"I've been up all night, sitting out here." Robert looked up from the book he was reading, *Huckleberry Finn*. "There were about a dozen of those flying squirrels darting around and although I hate to admit it, I was kind of scared."

Brandon told him how sorry he was about the squirrels. He said Robert's feet looked like they had never left the New York sidewalks. Mish never budged and was still sleeping.

I've recently redecorated the guesthouse pigeonnier as my own nesting spot while visiting Parlange. On the second floor, the nests for the birds are in their original state and are filled with our favorite books and old National Geographics. It's a very cozy space and I'm happy not to be underfoot. But guess who else thinks it's especially delightful? Ladybugs.

I don't know how God can make so many ladybugs. There are so many that it looks like the Red Sea. You sweep them up and after eight hours of sleep they're back again. I'm sorry to say this, but I now hate ladybugs. And no, they don't bring good luck—they are a nuisance. My mother told me ours are Chinese ladybugs that bite; I never knew ladybugs were so global.

After just a few weeks of being settled in, however, I've gotten used to being greeted with a warm welcome by the ladybugs. I'd take them any day over wasps or flying squirrels. I didn't mention that there are salamanders, too, which found a perfect home under the brick steps that Robert so enjoyed. At least they are outside.

Who knows what guests will be next? For the time being though, it's just me, my books, and the ladybugs. Chinese ladybugs.

THE FIRST FLOOR OF THE PIGEONNIER

Recipe For
LINEN AND RIBBON BEDSPREADS

LINEN AND RIBBON

1. Determine whether you are making a twin, full, queen, or king-size bedspread.

2. Go to a fabric store such as Joanne's Fabrics. Pick out your desired linen color and ask the salesclerk to determine the amount of fabric needed for your size bed. If desired, pick out a color for the piping (I chose the same color as the linen). Again, the salesclerk can help you determine the amount of fabric needed for the piping. Piping is cut on the bias and takes more yardage than one would expect. Although piping is not essential, it gives the piece a finished look.

3. Buy ribbon that will go around the entire border of the bedspread. Usually you don't have to do the side that doesn't show. In fact, I only bordered three sides because the ribbon was expensive and one side of both beds is against a wall. I bought my ribbon from the Promenade Fabric Store in New Orleans. The fabric is imported by Hyman Hendler in New York City, where it is also available. I also used an inner lining because I like the weight and the way the lining makes curtains and bedspreads drape. This is certainly not a requirement, however.

4. Usually an establishment that performs alterations can make this simple sort of piece. I suggest phoning a number of places until you find one who agrees to complete the project.

What I enjoy the most about this very simple bedspread is that it is custom-made. Although the bedspread costs about the same as ordering one from a catalog, it is a unique creation that no one else will have.

Part Five
LITTLE COCKTAIL DRESSES
FOR THE HOME

#F207
CROWN

#CC309
SANTECROCE
8 X 16

#F203
BRUMIERE
16 X 16

#F206
ETOILE

#F205
THERMIDOR
8 X 16

#F202
FLOREAL
16 X 16

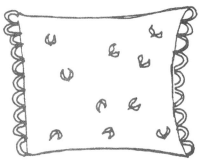

#F201
VENTOSE
16 X 16

#M104
FAIRGROUND
18 X 18 BOX

#M105
METROPOLITIAN
18 X 18

MY COLLECTION OF SILK DUPIONI CUSHIONS

Upon seeing my first collection of cushions,

furniture designer Mario Villa said, "They're little cocktail dresses for the home." He knew that I had been a dress designer and that the cushions—trimmed in passementerie and fabricated in jewel-tone silk dupionis—were really inspired by my dresses. Rather than buy an entire new living room suite, I gave new life to a room with these little injections of color. It's not about throwing out everything old, but instead adding spice to your life and house—whether it is through color or accessories, or perhaps by showcasing a wonderful collection inspired by a hobby or passion. A chef I know collects old thermos bottles and displays them atop his cabinets in his minimalist kitchen. They, not the Viking stove or gourmet pots, are the centerpiece of his kitchen. Whatever suits your fancy or inspires you should be your M.O. in decorating. Then coming home really is *home, sweet home*.

LITTLE COCKTAIL DRESSES
FOR THE HOME

⟶⟡ ⟡⟵

When people ask me what I like to do, I never, ever say shopping. Ever.

But when I am out shopping, it's not so much that I want to buy everything that I see, but rather that the amazing mixture of textures, color, and shapes intrigues me. This visual sensation truly revs me up and gets my adrenaline flowing. In fact, the first cushion that I ever made was inspired by a skirt I had designed; the second cushion by a pair of shoes I bought in London.

Who knew that the black velvet cocktail skirt I had studded and trimmed with looped-jet beaded balls would become the inspiration for my entire cushion collection? Although I didn't make my first pillows in black velvet or trim them in jet beading, which might have been appropriate for Storyville (a New Orleans area started in 1898 where jazz originated as the entertainment for the bordellos, lavishly decorated clubs offering women of ill-repute. Storyville was declared illegal in 1917 and closed down by the federal government), the jewel-toned silk dupioni cushions were embellished with looped balls just like the cocktail skirt. The balls used for the pillows were antique hair-net and bronze doré fringed balls found at the Marché aux Puces at Port de Clignancourt, one of my favorite flea markets outside of Paris. This sort of passementerie was originally used for fancy courtesan curtains. Although I only had a limited inventory of these trimmings, I was able to locate very similar pieces at a place called Tinsel Trading in New York's garment district. The owner, Marcia Ceppos, makes frequent trips to France and brings back beautiful trimmings for her shop. Tinsel Trim and Hyman Hendler, just down the block from Tinsel Trading, and a wonderful European ribbon importer, are two of my favorite resources. They are shrines to me.

OPPOSITE: SHOPPING AT HERITAGE ANTIQUES IN NEW ROADS, LOUISIANA

The other hit in my cushion collection was inspired by a pair of black suede loafers I bought in London. These classically designed shoes had a square toe good for walking and a stiff, vertical, black suede knot attached to the top of the heel that brushed against the ankle. The knot created the effect of a black seam on a pair of fishnet panty hose. I decided to have Khanh, my ace seamstress, copy the knot in dupioni and weave in gold rope cording; I wanted to see what the knot would look like as a sort-of-trim for the cushions. Once Khanh got the knot right, I had her space the knots evenly on a pillow. Rather than stud the pillow with antique hairnet balls, I dotted little gold charms in classical icons: crowns, fleur-de-lis, reeds, a Florentine lily, and other similar motifs. Again, the landscapes for the crown jewels were vivid hues of aubergine, magenta, gold, rouge, lavender, and other colors dear to my heart. Luckily

for me and my business, these cushions had a cult following, and unlike the dresses I designed, were one size fits all. There were no busts, waists, or hips to worry about.

On my last trip to New York, I wanted to say "hi" to Marcia. Tinsel Trading's window display has remained the same since I first shopped there in 1992. Marcia says that she doesn't even bother to clean the windows because they'll just get all sooty again. I had assumed that with all the user-friendly inventory software available now she couldn't help but organize that chaotic system of hers. Yet I have to say that every shipment I receive from her is perfectly packaged with exactly what I ordered.

I walked in, and, as usual, there was Marcia acting as cashier. The store looked exactly the same with more curious fringe piled on top of older inventory. Marcia told me I'd have to wait for her to check out her customer and then she'd help me. I watched her handwrite the sale and pierce it through an old-fashioned ice-pick receipt holder. Then she moved from behind the counter and whispered to me, "Would you like to come upstairs (off limits) to see what I brought back from Paris?" That offer was much better than the satisfaction I would get from a new pair of Jimmy Choo boots.

Birds-eye View. PORT CHESTER, N. Y.

Monsieur L. Seignette

à La Rochelle.

Happy
New Year

UNLOADING BANANAS, FROM SHIP SIDE
NEW ORLEANS, LA.

MORE OLD-FASHIONED POSTCARDS

10071. EAGLE NEST ROCK, GARDINER CANYON, YELLOWSTONE PARK.

Haynes-Photo.

INTERIOR OF ST. LOUIS CATHEDRAL
NEW ORLEANS, LOUISIANA

17243. SHOSHONE DAM—328 FT., YELLOWSTONE NATIONAL PARK.

8169. Biscuit Basin, Yellowstone National Park.

THE YELLOWSTONE, YELLOWSTONE NATIONAL PARK.

CABILDO

ST. LOUIS CATHEDRAL

STATE HISTORICAL MUSEUM

JACKSON MONUMENT

PONTALBA APARTMENTS

Jackson Square, New Orleans, La.

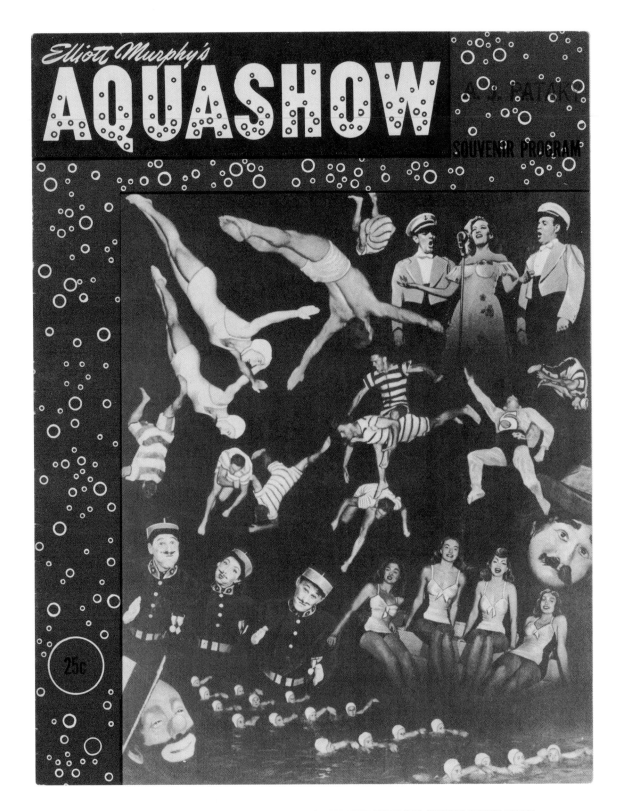

PROGRAM COVER FOR THE AQUASHOW. ANOTHER FUN PIECE FOR FUTURE INSPIRATION.

COMB

TAJ
Luxury Hotels

TOOTHBRUSH PACKAGING FROM
THE TAJ HOTEL IN BOMBAY, INDIA.
THIS IS THE KIND OF SOUVENIR I
BRING HOME FOR COLOR IDEAS.

I'M A DADDY!

THE NURSE SAYS THERE ARE
TWO!

THREE!

FOUR!

A SET OF ANTIQUE CARDS
THAT COULD INFLUENCE
A NEW PROJECT

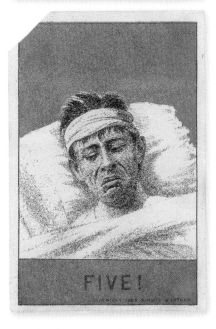

FIVE!

FROM LEFT: KHANH TRAN, ME, AND
HUONG PHAM IN FRONT OF THEIR
SHOP, THIMBELINA

HELP WANTED

Everything was in place to start my dress-designing business: I had the fashion design talent, the iridescent silk taffeta, the jeweled buttons and trim, lining, seam binding, needles, thread, and commercial sewing machines. But there was one thing missing: seamstresses. Not just any old seamstresses either. I had tried out every good seamstress in New Orleans East- and Westbank. No use. None of them were good enough, and if they were, they could only make one of anything. What I needed was manufacturing, on a small scale, but with couture quality.

After exhausting all of my resources, I called the Association of Catholic Charities. Mrs. Benhana, the head of the association, told me that her organization was in charge of finding jobs for Vietnamese workers, many of whom were excellent seamstresses in need of work. She arranged for me to meet Father Dominique Maithanh Luong of Maria Nu Voung Vietnam Catholic Church. He was delighted with my interest in his parishioners.

My plan was simple: Make a poster-board sign saying, in Vietnamese, "SKILLED SEAMSTRESSES WANTED." Tu, my neighborhood Vietnamese grocer, would do the translation for me. I would stand outside the church on a Sunday with my sign and wait for Mass to let out.

This was the first time I had ever been on-time for Mass, and it was my first trip to New Orleans East, also called "Little Saigon." I sat in my car and watched all of the churchgoers in their Sunday clothes enter church. When I assumed communion was taking place, I got out of my car and positioned myself a few feet from the church's stained glass exit doors. Holding my poster-board sign handwritten by Tu in black magic marker, along with a white ruled pad marked with the following columns: **Name, Address, Telephone, Can/cannot drive, Have/have no car** (these last two columns were almost as important as sewing), and an attached four-color Bic Clic, I couldn't have been more ready.

Father Dominique led the procession of acolytes and parishioners out of church singing "Bring the Labor On." I recognized the hymn, but not the Vietnamese words, and felt right at home. That was, until I saw a group of women with their shiny black hair squinting at my sign. The women whispered to each other and smiled with their large white teeth . . . and then they barraged me. I could hardly keep up with my list and keeping them in queue. It wasn't just the women; men were just as eager to sign my list. Father Dominique and an English-speaking acolyte saw that I was swamped and came to my assistance. I was on the third page of my legal pad when the last signer left. Surely five of those seventy-five could sew to my expectations. Father Dominique offered me the use of the parish hall for our meeting place next Wednesday after midweek Eucharist. He said that a number of the parishioners met for a sort of sewing club after Wednesday Mass, and that they would have samples to show me.

I could hardly wait for Wednesday.

Wednesday arrived, and so did I, at St. Maria Catholic Church Parish Hall. I was early. They were earlier. When I walked into the room, they all smiled and held up their samples: beige double-knit trousers with the sewn-in, personalized labels that you can buy in a pack at a sewing shop. Each of their sample trousers read: "Handmade with love by Khanh," "Handmade with love by Huong," "Handmade with love by Loan," or "Handmade with love by Harry." I asked Harry how come he had an English name. "My real name Huong; call me Harry," he replied.

Then there was a group of ladies with samples of large, peach-and-mauve-colored silk flowers which they thought were very pretty. Each flower had a label that could have been a first cousin to the trouser sewers' label: "Handmade with love from Mommy."

This wasn't exactly what I thought the sewing club's talent would be, although their workmanship was very detailed, neat, and precise: the making of a good seamstress.

But when I inquired if any of them had ever made dresses, they answered no. With that response I knew that I would have to call in a professional pattern maker to train them.

Louisiana State University has a wonderful home economics department. Although the school is an hour and a half away, I felt sure that I could find someone. A professor who was head of the department, and an expert pattern maker, agreed to consult. Elva came to New Orleans on several occasions to train the women—the men didn't want to make dresses.

Khanh and Loan, the head seamstresses, used Wolf model forms (an industry standard), and me for the samples. They always said, "Ange (the name of the dress line, a combination of my former partner Jeanne's and my names, and their nickname for me, too), you about a size ten."

"I'm not a size ten!" I would shriek. "I'm a two."

But to the seamstresses and their diminutive size, I was a ten and I had to think of that number in a more positive light, like on a scale of one to ten.

The ladies initially sewed from their homes. While waiting for orders to be completed, I would sample the delicious egg rolls they made for their families. I even tried to make myself eat their fish soup, but instead opted to help the children with their multiplication tables. The only problem with this home-sewing arrangement was that when it came time to ship the Neiman Marcus order, the dresses reeked of egg rolls. We had to delay the shipment a day while the clothes aired out.

Once the orders grew, I set up a workroom in New Orleans East where we could all collaborate together. I commuted from Uptown New Orleans to Little Saigon by car; they rode on nearly new bicycles I purchased for them from the New Orleans Police Department. The seamstresses could even walk to work because they lived so close to the workroom. Even though it was a drag of a commute for me (30 minutes to and from), and not very scenic, there was an amazing Vietnamese vegetable and fruit market nearby. I learned many Vietnamese customs and the seamstresses and I shared many meals together. In return, I helped them with their studies to become citizens of our country. When the Anjé dresses said, "Made in the USA," that meant more than just, "Handmade with love by Khanh." Those dresses had voting rights, too.

"It's not D.I.Y,

it's D.D.I.Y.

Tom Sawyer had

this figured out a long

time ago."

NEGOTIATING WITH ROCIO SALAS

MY BEDROOM AND FOUR-POSTER BED IN NEW ORLEANS

FENG SHUI, SHOES, AND LIQUOR

❖

"Alton," I asked, "could you wait until I phone William, my architect friend, to discuss what corner I should put the bed in?"

"Take as long as you want," Alton said. "This is my first trip to New Orleans and all I'm supposed to do is deliver this here bed to you and help you move anything you need."

Alton was a jack-of-all-trades who worked for my father. He had been looking forward to this day because he was a curious person who reveled in an adventure. Although Alton had never been to New Orleans, which was two hours away from Parlange, he said that he'd find his way there without a map or directions. And he did, without any difficulty. When he saw the Superdome from the interstate, he said it was like the Second Coming. And when he saw the cemeteries with the above-ground graves, he really thought something was happening.

I could tell he was a little rattled as he drove up to my house and got out of his truck; he had taken in a lot of religion during his trip. The two of us brought in the pieces of the four-poster spool bed from my childhood. The walnut bed dates back to around 1850. I wanted to replace my original blue-and-white patchwork quilt, white

THE FOUR-POSTER BED AND TEESTER AT PARLANGE
LONG BEFORE I INHERITED IT

Battenberg pillows, and calico bolster with an updated bed dressing. The new bed outfit was a white piqué bedspread with embroidered aqua crowns inspired by my great-great-grandmother's calling card. I recovered my aqua silk dupioni and Spanish moss-hair-stuffed bolster (made from the Spanish moss that grows on live oak trees in Louisiana) and trimmed it with white marabou.

Whenever Alton said hello to you or agreed with you, he bent over with his hands folded and took a little bow—just like a praying mantis. I had seen him greet his wife Clara this way, too. Even though she had just died, Alton was always smiling and whistling " Brown-Eyed Girl."

"William told me to try facing the bed away from the sun," I told Alton, who moved the bed to the shady side of the room. "I'm going to wait and see how this feels."

"No problem," he said, with a chewed cigar hanging from his lip. "I'm going to start moving these shoes from up under this bed."

After about an hour of circling and contemplating the bed's location, we took a lunch break. Driving in Alton's white Ford 250 pickup truck, we headed to Domilise's Po'boys and Bar on Annunciation Street. Alton ordered a combination roast beef and fried shrimp po'boy with gravy and I had my usual half oyster, half shrimp po'boy. We ordered a Barq's root beer while we waited for our order.

"This is dee-li-cious," Alton squealed. He made a funny high-pitched squeal or yell whenever he was excited; it was his trademark. "I only wish I could tell Clara about this bread when I get home," he said. "She always liked to hear about any new dishes I had so she could try to make them herself," he said, putting his head down and closing his eyes.

"You and all of us are going to miss her," I said, looking across the table at him.

"Yep, but I'll tell her about the Superdome and cemeteries when we meet in heaven, and that'll make her so happy. By the way, we forgot to say the blessing. I'll say it for the two of us now."

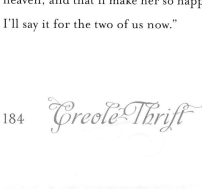

MY J'AIME L'AMOUR FABRIC DESIGN
TRIMMED WITH BOAS

We bowed our heads as he thanked God for letting him see New Orleans and have his first po'boy. But he prayed he wouldn't be buried in New Orleans, closing with "AMEN!"

After lunch, we stopped at Hansen's Sno-Bliz on Tchoupitoulas Street for a snow-ball. As usual, there was a line, but Alton was not in any hurry to leave New Orleans. After we sipped our cream of nectar snowballs, we drove over potholes in Alton's four-wheel-drive truck back to my house and the bed dilemma. "Those potholes are worser than those big old ant piles in the pasture."

"Alton, would you mind moving the bed to face the sun?" He pushed the bed to the other corner. This angle felt good to me, but again, I paced around the room to see if I got a warm, cozy feeling. Meanwhile, Alton continued to move more shoes. When he was finished with the shoes, he went into the kitchen. Although he was not in sight, I heard bottles and glasses clanking. Maybe he was rearranging my kitchen cabinets. He always looked for things to do and I bet he wanted to see what I kept in my pantry. The sun was beginning to set and the light was just right in the room. "I want to leave the bed here."

"Okay, if you're sure, then I'll put the teester (a frame originally used for hanging mosquito nets to protect one while sleeping) on top of the four posters."

"Do it now so I won't change my mind, please," I said laughing.

It was time for me to make my bed. I put the coverlet and bolster in place, but there was still something missing. Originally, fabric had covered the teester in a sunburst design, but now the fabric had been removed and the teester was just an empty frame. A leftover bolt of silk metallic organza from a dress I had made leaned against the wall. I cut two long lengths of it and draped them across the teester. That looked good.

"Reach in my red tool box and hand me my staple gun, please, Alton." I stapled the two pieces of fabric to the teester frame.

I remembered the small crystal chandelier I'd bought in London, which was stored in my sauna. After unwrapping the melted bubble wrap from the chandelier, I held it in the middle of the teester. "Could you get a hook for this chandelier and hang it from the teester's center board?" I asked. Alton got the hook, drilled a little hole, hung the chandelier, and plugged the extension cord into the wall. "Hit the light switch."

"That sure beats that itty-bitty night light they advertise at Wal-Mart," he said.

When Alton got home, my father was waiting outside on the gallery looking concerned. "I've been worried about you," he said. It couldn't have taken you that long to haul that bed to New Orleans."

"I had to wait on Angèle to decide what corner of the room she wanted to place the bed."

"She must've had other things to move," he said, removing his straw cowboy hat and scratching his head.

"Mainly shoes and liquor, Mr. Junior."

OPPOSITE: MY GUEST ROOM

THE GUEST ROOM VANITY

Recipe For
"Feng Sui, Shoes, and Liquor": Piqué Bedspread with Embroidered Crown Motif

WHITE COTTON PIQUE (YARDAGE DEPENDS ON BED SIZE),
SILK DUPIONI FOR PIPING

1. Determine the size of the bedspread—twin, full, queen, or king. These are standard measurements.

2. Go to a fabric store such as Joanne's Fabrics, and select white cotton pique. Cotton pique comes in different patterns (i.e., bird's-eye is what I chose). Ask the salesclerk to help you determine the amount of fabric needed for your bed size. Pick out a color for the piping; I chose aqua silk dupioni. The salesclerk can also help you determine the amount of piping needed.

3. Usually, an establishment that performs alterations can make this simple sort of piece. I suggest phoning a number of places until you find one that agrees to complete the project.

4. *Once the bedspread is made, decide whether you would like a monogram or image (a crown for me) and take the bedspread to an establishment that creates monograms. There is a place in New Orleans called Monogram Express which can tackle almost any design. With the rampant monogram trend, it's easy to find a company who can perform this step for you.*

5. *I chose to have my crown spaced evenly in the center of the spread and embroidered in the same aqua color as my piping.*

6. *The end result gave me such joy—the coverlet felt very personal with my crown design. Even though it isn't my monogram, it's the closest I'll ever get to a tattoo.*

RESOURCES

ANN KOERNER ANTIQUES
4021 Magazine Street
New Orleans, Louisiana 70115
504-895-2664

ARTISTIC FRAME
985 Third Avenue
New York, New York 10022
212-289-2100

A great place to find chair frames including Louis XV and XVI styles; catalog available.

BELL'OCCHIO
8 Brady Street
San Francisco, California 94103
415-864-4048
www.bellocchio.com

One of my favorite shops in the United States, Bell'ochio sells French ribbon, ephemera, wrapping paper, old love letters and calling cards, curiosities. You're bound to be inspired upon entering the store or browsing online.

BERGERON PECANS
New Roads, Louisiana 70760
225-638-9626

The best pecans from Pointe Coupée Parish.

CONCRETE IMPRESSIONIST, C I CONSTRUCTION & DESIGN
678 Benjamin Street
Brooklyn, New York 11208-5304
718-677-1298

A source for the concrete table top.

HERITAGE ANTIQUES
116 W. Main Street
New Roads, Louisiana
225-618-1000

HYMAN HENDLER & SONS
67 W. 38th Street
New York, New York 10018
212-840-8393

Sells ribbon and passementerie.

JO-ANN'S FABRIC
www.joann.com for store locations and for ordering online. Jo-Ann's stores are located in almost every city.

JOHN ROBSHAW
245 W. 29th Street
New York, New York 10001
212-594-6006

Sells the fabric featured on the settee in the pigeonnier.

KATIE KOCH
Discerning Fabric Solutions
1125 Josephine Street
New Orleans, Louisiana 70130
504-410-1450

The best New Orleans establishment for curtain making and other decorative creations including coverlets, pillows, and most of all, Katie's eye.

KINKO'S/FEDEX
www.fedex.com for store locations.

LAKEVIEW ANTIQUES
6020 Wye Road
Lakeland, Louisiana 70752
225-627-6197

THE LIBRARY OF CONGRESS
   AMERICAN MEMORY
101 Independence Avenue SE
Washington, D.C. 20540
http://rs6.loc.gov

A wonderful source for old photographs, maps, literature, and architecture in the public domain. Most photographs can be purchased online from $25 and up for a black-and-white photograph.

M & J TRIMMING
1008 Avenue of the Americas
New York, New York 10018
212-391-9072
mjtrim.com

MARIA DE LABARRE
Pass Christian, Mississippi
228-547-8046
cake_diva_2004@yahoo.com

Maria created the birthday cake featured in the Zodiac birthday party story.

PJ'S COFFEE
5432 Magazine Street
New Orleans, Louisiana 70115
504-899-2190
www.pjscoffee.com

PROMENADE FINE FABRICS
1520 St. Charles Avenue
New Orleans, Louisiana 70130
504-522-1488

SAGE STREET ANTIQUES
114 Division Street
Sag Harbor, New York 11963
631-725-4036

TENDER BUTTONS
143 E. 62nd Street
New York, New York 10021
212-758-7004

The best selection of unique antique buttons.

THIMBELINA
5720 Magazine Street
New Orleans, Louisiana 70115
504-895-5700

My original workroom and the most beloved employees, Khanh Tran and Hung Pham.

They can create almost anything with your vision.

TINSEL TRADING COMPANY
47 W. 38th Street
New York, New York 10018
212-730-1030 (Marcia Ceppos)
www.TinselTrading.com

TODDY MAKER
888-863-3974
www.Toddycafe.com

For the New Orleans Ice Coffee recipe.

WINE SELLER BY BEN LAZICH
5000 Prytania Street
New Orleans, Louisiana 70115
504-895-3828

Carries the pechaud bitters featured in the Sazerac recipe.

from PLANTATION KITCHENS

"BELLE GROVE" BARBECUE SAUCE. Into a saucepan, put 1 large onion and 1 green pepper, both chopped, with 1½ cups of tomato juice, 1 cup of vinegar, ½ cup of tomato ketchup, ¼ cup of Worcestershire sauce, ¼ cup of beefsteak sauce, ½ cup of butter and 1 teaspoon of salt. Simmer ½ hour. Serve on hamburgers.

"SUNSET" PECAN PIE. Lightly stir together the following, adding them in the order given: 1 cup of white syrup, ½ cup of sugar (¼ white, ¼ brown), 3 teaspoons of flour, 2 eggs, 1 teaspoon of vanilla extract, 1 cup of pecan meat pieces. Don't beat the eggs. Pour into an unbaked crust with...

"PARLA...
earthenw...
young lo...
of parbo...
of the oy...
peppers, ...
the fish, ...
the pie d...

"WINDY...
ing point...
spoons o...
ginger r...
sifted flo...
nately. N...
powder. ...
sauce in ...

LOUISIA...
and fry b...
a kettle a...
ready 2 q...
of flour. ...
stirring c...
adding m...
a sieve. ...
highly w...

SCALLO...
spoon of ...
1 cup of ...
When bre...
1 cup of ...
hard boil...
and bake...

"Belle Grove" · *Louisiana* · *Garland* · *"Sunset"* · *"Parlange"* · *"Oak Alley"*

Mr. James Reynolds, artist, designer and epicure, recently visited Louisiana, fell in love with the old houses along the bayous and with the food their cooks prepared. He came back with a sheaf of drawings, a notebook full of recipes which he wove together into a Louisiana Garland for our readers

MR. AND MRS. WALTER C. PARLANGE
MR. AND MRS. NELSON S. WOODDY
REQUEST YOUR PRESENCE
AT A PLANTATION PARTY

IN HONOR OF

MISS HAVARD EWIN
MISS ANNE KILPATRICK
MISS MARY ZIEGLER

SUNDAY, OCTOBER THE TWENTIETH
PARLANGE PLANTATION

12 O'CLOCK NOON   R. S. V. P.
                      5708 GARFIELD ST.

DIRECTIONS

TAKE AIRLINE HIGHWAY FROM NEW ORLEANS TO BATON ROUGE; CROSS NEW BRIDGE OVER MISSISSIPPI RIVER AT BATON ROUGE; PROCEED WEST ON HIGHWAY NO. 71-190 TO FORK IN ROAD; TURN RIGHT AT FORK ON TO CONCRETE HIGHWAY NO. 93 TO PARLANGE PLANTATION. PARLANGE PLANTATION FACES FALSE RIVER & IS SIX (6) MILES THIS SIDE OF NEW ROADS. IT IS APPROXIMATELY 110 MILES BY ROAD FROM NEW ORLEANS.

New Roads · Parlange Plantation · Fork: Turn Right Onto Road 93 · New Bridge Over Miss. · Baton Rouge · Air Line Highway · New Orls. · N

AFTERWORD

OCTOBER 5, 2005

I wonder if there was an odor that permeated after the Civil War? Literally and figuratively, I want to know now, especially, because all I can think of is the smell of rotten garbage, or far worse, sun-baked fish, that I smelled upon arriving at Louis Armstrong airport this morning. It's my first visit back since Katrina. The hours of CNN, Fox News, ABC, NBC, and CBS I've been watching have not prepared me for this scenery. At all. The Japanese magnolias that bloom at this time of year are postponed—to an undetermined date. Jasmine, ginger, and cape jasmine, my favorite New Orleans fragrances, have all been replaced with the rancid smell of old iceboxes thrown along the curb. Piles of them.

❖ ❖ ❖

To think that I left Louisiana on August 23 for a photo shoot in Manhattan and a birthday party in Sag Harbor on what would become the night of Hurricane Katrina, and now here I am, back in the city that bore me and my career. I have a better idea of what my great-great-grandmother must have felt when all she built and treasured—successful cotton and sugarcane crops, her portraits and beautiful furniture and gardens—was gone overnight. Yet she had the will to move on and make do with what she DID have. The difference is that I only lost my roof. Others lost everything. Everything except their spirit.

So much of what I have designed and created is thanks to the fabric and eccentricities of New Orleans and its people. From picking up far-flung colleagues, journalists, and friends at the airport with to-go cups (until recently, even the driver could have one) of Milk Punch or Vodka Gimlets

197

from Mr. B's and Peristyle, then heading to Vaughn's or Joe's Cozy Cub to hear my friend Kermit Ruffin play his trumpet while eating red beans and rice (included in the $5 cover)—all so easy to provide. And now to re-create this triptych, I'm not sure where I would begin. Naturally, the drive-thru daiquiri bars are up and running again even though there's no potable water in the entire city.

This book's spirit, the adventures, places, and characters, all hail from what so many call "the most European city in America." When my friend Lydia's seven-year-old son decided he'd like to go to Paris, she replied, "How about New Orleans? It's just a train ride away." George's tall order was fulfilled. Indeed. New Orleans is without a doubt a place where people who want to leave their troubles behind choose as home. It's gracious, forgiving, and accepting, and those rare qualities are why it will come back stronger than ever. If there were ever a template for my "Creole Thrift," the renewal of New Orleans would be a textbook example. That is why this book is dedicated to the mighty Mississippi and its Crescent City.

Creole Thrift

ACKNOWLEDGMENTS

Four men sheltered me from the storm (Katrina): William Waldron, my brilliant photographer, during the calm before it; Richard Keith Langham, during it; Steven Gambrel and Chris Connor, after it. Without Keith's ability to keep me in stitches even in the midst of such a tragedy, and Steven and Chris's beautiful Sag Harbor guest house and perfect backdrop for writing, this book and I might have been in the self-help section. Although my friend David Ebner, who made my soap-on-a-rope, says he always meets the cutest girls in the self-help aisle. So that wouldn't have been so bad.

Instead, Lydia Somerville, thank you for convincing William Waldron that he *had* to do the book, or else, and the grand time we had shooting it and learning a lesson or two from him. Thanks to James Nolan, my talented writing teacher and all my classmates, especially John D. Gray, for your ongoing commentary and for teaching me that ghosts *do* exist; Melissa, his delightful wife and gifted writer for teaching me not to give away the suspense; Desirée Petitbon, for our early morning meetings of the minds; Chris Bynum for helping Stella get her groove back; Vicki Morgan, my first editor and the real land lady; and Adelaide Russo, my genius French professor friend who has been an eyewitness to it all and labeled me "unpredictable". . . fun and adventure. Thank goodness she clarified that.

Thank you Robert Valley, for your flair and ability to win everyone's heart at Parlange and make it and all of us look better; Katherine Slingluff, you may have assisted William but you sure can play the ukulele; and Susan Schadt and Mimi Davis, the big sisters I never had, for your shower and good sense. I am most grateful to Peggy Brown, a.k.a. Uptown Chocolate Brown, and Betty Reck for your wisdom and our book club, and Susan Schadt and Mimi Davis, the big sisters I never had, for our shopping triumphs and for always being right.

Deborah Davis, for your insisting that I have "just coffee" with Wendy Silbert, who would become my literary agent and treasured friend; and to Harvey Klinger, both of the Harvey Klinger Agency, who inherited me—in spades: Thank you. And to Robyn Liverant, thanks for making things happen.

Claire Dishman, you taught me to be on time. Christina Wressell, thank you for the chicken coop and your comical self and Mish, for embellishing me with beautiful jewelry and friendship. The same goes for the jewelry designer Elizabeth Locke plus the roof she has provided over the years.

And thanks to Judith Regan for pursuing me and believing in my work; Cassie Jones and Maureen O'Neal, my editor, thank goodness you're half Southern as only you could understand the Cat's Meow slipcover lady; Jenny Brown and Kurt Andrews, whom I knew I could always count on being at a meeting.

Last, but so not least, my gratitude to New Orleans and all who have supported my business. Without the Crescent City attached to my name, I'd just be another girl next door.

OPPOSITE AND NEXT SPREAD: INTERIOR OF GAMAY RESTAURANT,
WHICH ARCHITECT WILLIAM SONNER AND I DESIGNED.